A SURGEON IN BELGIUM

The Nursing Staff, Furnes.

A SURGEON IN BELGIUM

BY

H. S. SOUTTAR, F.R.C.S.

ASSISTANT SURGEON, WEST LONDON HOSPITAL
LATE SURGEON-IN-CHIEF, BELGIAN FIELD HOSPITAL

ILLUSTRATED

The Naval & Military Press Ltd

Published by

The Naval & Military Press Ltd
Unit 10 Ridgewood Industrial Park,
Uckfield, East Sussex,
TN22 5QE England

Tel: +44 (0) 1825 749494
Fax: +44 (0) 1825 765701

www.naval-military-press.com
www.military-genealogy.com

In reprinting in facsimile from the original, any imperfections are inevitably reproduced and the quality may fall short of modern type and cartographic standards.

TO
THE BRAVE SOLDIERS OF BELGIUM

PREFACE

To write the true story of three months' work in a hospital is a task before which the boldest man might quail. Let my very dear friends of the Belgian Field Hospital breathe again, for I have attempted nothing of the sort. I would sooner throw aside my last claim to self-respect, and write my autobiography. It would at least be safer. But there were events which happened around us, there was an atmosphere in which we lived, so different from those of our lives at home that one felt compelled to try to picture them before they merged into the shadowy memories of the past. And this is all that I have attempted.

To all who worked with me through those months I owe a deep debt of gratitude. That they would do everything in their power to make the hospital a success went without saying, but it was quite another matter that they should all have conspired to make the time for me one of the happiest upon which I shall ever look back. Where all have been so kind, it is almost invidious to mention names, and yet there are two which must stand by themselves. To the genius and the invincible resource of Madame Sindici the hospital owes an incalculable debt. Her friendship is one of my most delightful memories. The sterling powers of Dr. Beavis brought us safely many a time through deep water, and but for his enterprise the hospital would have come to an abrupt conclusion with Antwerp. There could have been no more delightful colleague, and without his aid much of this book would never have been written.

For the Belgian Field Hospital I can wish nothing better than that its star may continue to shine in the future as it has always done in the past, and that a sensible British public may generously support the most enterprising hospital in the war.

H. S. S.

CONTENTS

		PAGE
I.	TO ANTWERP	1
II.	THE HOSPITAL	11
III.	THE DAY'S WORK	19
IV.	ANTWERP	32
V.	TERMONDE	42
VI.	THE CHÂTEAU	50
VII.	MALINES	61
VIII.	LIERRE	68
IX.	A PAUSE	79
X.	THE SIEGE	85
XI.	CONTICH	93
XII.	THE BOMBARDMENT—NIGHT	104
XIII.	THE BOMBARDMENT—DAY	110
XIV.	THE NIGHT JOURNEY	120
XV.	FURNES	128
XVI.	POPERINGHE	137
XVII.	FURNES AGAIN	147
XVIII.	WORK AT FURNES	156
XIX.	FURNES—THE TOWN	166
XX.	A JOURNEY	174
XXI.	THE AMBULANCE CORPS	181
XXII.	PERVYSE—THE TRENCHES	190
XXIII.	YPRES	199
XXIV.	SOME CONCLUSIONS	211

LIST OF ILLUSTRATIONS

	FACING PAGE
THE NURSING STAFF, FURNES	*Frontispiice*
A WARD AT ANTWERP	12
AN OPERATION AT ANTWERP	22
THE DIRECTOR, DR. BEAVIS, AT ANTWERP	36
TERMONDE	46
LIERRE	74
HOMELESS	96
ANTWERP—AFTER THE BOMBARDMENT	116
THE SURGICAL STAFF, FURNES	128
DINNER—FURNES	132
THE COURTYARD, FURNES	132
THE LAUNDRY, FURNES	144
MAURICE	152
A STRAW WARD, FURNES	152
MADAME CURIE	162
ST. WALBURGA, FURNES	166
YPRES	194
PERVYSE	194
THE CLOTH HALL, YPRES, AFTER BOMBARDMENT	202

A SURGEON IN BELGIUM

I

TO ANTWERP

WHEN, one Saturday afternoon in September, we stepped on board the boat for Ostend, it was with a thrill of expectation. For weeks we had read and spoken of one thing only—the War—and now we were to see it for ourselves, we were even in some way to be a part of it. The curtain was rising for us upon the greatest drama in all the lurid history of strife. We should see the armies as they went out to fight, and we should care for the wounded when their work was done. We might hear the roar of the guns and the scream of the shells. To us, that was War.

And, indeed, we have seen more of war in these few weeks than has fallen to the lot of many an old campaigner. We have been through the siege of Antwerp, we have lived and worked always close to the firing-line, and I have seen a great cruiser roll over and sink, the victim of a submarine. But these are not the things which will live in our minds. These things are the mere framing of the grim picture. The cruiser has been blotted out by the weary faces of an endless stream of fugitives, and the scream of the shells has been drowned by the cry of a child. For, though the soldiers may fight, it is the people who suffer, and the toll of war is not the life which it takes, but the life which it destroys.

I suppose, and I hope, that there is not a man amongst us who has not in his heart wished to go to the front, and to do what he could. The thought may have been only transitory, and may soon have been blotted out by self-interest; and there is many a strong man who has thrust it from him because he knew that his duty lay at home. But to everyone the wish must have come, though only to a few can come the opportunity. We all want to do our share, but it is only human that we should at the same time long to be there in the great business of the hour, to see war as it really is, to feel the thrill of its supreme moments, perhaps in our heart of hearts to make quite certain that we are not cowards. And when we return, what do we bring with us? We all bring a few bits of shell, pictures of ruined churches, perhaps a German helmet—and our friends are full of envy. And some of us return with scenes burnt into our brain of horror and of pathos such as no human pen can describe. Yet it is only when we sit down in the quiet of our homes that we realize the deeper meaning of all that we have seen, that we grasp the secret of the strange aspects of humanity which have passed before us. What we have seen is a world in which the social conventions under which we live, and which form a great part or the whole of most of our lives, have been torn down. Men and women are no longer limited by the close barriers of convention. They must think and act for themselves, and for once it is the men and women that we see, and not the mere symbols which pass as coin in a world at peace. To the student of men and women, the field of war is the greatest opportunity in the world. It is a veritable dissecting-room, where all the queer machinery that goes to the making of us lies open to our view. On the whole, I am very glad that I am a mere surgeon, and that I can limit my dissections to men's bodies. Human Anatomy is bad enough, but after the last three months the mere thought of an analysis of Human Motives fills me with terror.

Our boat was one of the older paddle steamers. We were so fortunate as to have a friend at Court, and the best cabins on the ship were placed at our disposal. I was very grateful to that friend, for it was very rough, and our paddle-boxes were often under water. We consoled ourselves by the thought that at least in a rough sea we were safe from submarines, but the consolation became somewhat threadbare as time went on. Gradually the tall white cliffs of Dover sank behind us, splendid symbols of the quiet power which guards them. But for those great white cliffs, and the waves which wash their base, how different the history of England would have been! They broke the power of Spain in her proudest days, Napoleon gazed at them in vain as at the walls of a fortress beyond his grasp, and against them Germany will fling herself to her own destruction. Germany has yet to learn the strength which lies concealed behind those cliffs, the energy and resource which have earned for England the command of the sea. It was a bad day for Germany when she ventured to question that command. She will receive a convincing answer to her question.

We reached Ostend, and put up for the night at the Hôtel Terminus. Ostend was empty, and many of the hotels were closed. A few bombs had been dropped upon the town some days before, and caused considerable excitement—about all that most bombs ever succeed in doing, as we afterwards discovered. But it had been enough to cause an exodus. No one dreamt that in less than three weeks' time the town would be packed with refugees, and that to get either a bed or a meal would be for many of them almost impossible. Everywhere we found an absolute confidence as to the course of the war, and the general opinion was that the Germans would be driven out of Belgium in less than six weeks.

Two of our friends in Antwerp had come down to meet us by motor, and we decided to go back with them by road, as trains, though still running, were slow and uncertain. It was a terrible day, pouring in torrents and blowing a hurricane. Our route lay through Bruges and Ghent, but the direct road to Bruges was in a bad condition, and we chose the indirect road through Blankenberghe. We left Ostend by the magnificent bridge, with its four tall columns, which opens the way towards the north-east, and as we crossed it I met the first symbol of war. A soldier stepped forward, and held his rifle across our path. My companion leaned forward and murmured, "Namur," the soldier saluted, and we passed on. It was all very simple, and, but for the one word, silent; but it was the first time I had heard a password, and it made an immense impression on my mind. We had crossed the threshold of War. I very soon had other things to think about. The road from Ostend to Blankenberghe is about the one good motor road in Belgium, and my companion evidently intended to demonstrate the fact to me beyond all possibility of doubt. We were driving into the teeth of a squall, but there seemed to be no limits to the power of his engine. I watched the hand of his speedometer rise till it touched sixty miles per hour. On the splendid asphalt surface of the road there was no vibration, but a north-east wind across the sand-dunes is no trifle, and I was grateful when we turned south-eastwards at Blankenberghe, and I could breathe again.

As I said, that road by the dunes is unique. The roads of Belgium, for the most part, conform to one regular pattern. In the centre is a paved causeway, set with small stone blocks, whilst on each side is a couple of yards of loose sand, or in wet weather of deep mud. The causeway is usually only just wide enough for the passing of two motors, and on the smaller roads it is not sufficient even for this. As there is no speed limit, and everyone drives at the top power of his engine, the skill required to drive without mishap is considerable. After a little rain the stone is covered with a layer of greasy mud, and to keep a car upon it at a high speed is positively a gymnastic feat. In spite of every precaution, an occasional descent into the mud at the roadside is inevitable, and from that only a very powerful car can extricate itself with any ease. A small car will often have to slowly push its way out backwards. In dry weather the conditions are almost as bad, for often the roadside is merely loose sand, which gives no hold for a wheel. For a country so damp and low-lying as Belgium, there is probably nothing to equal a paved road, but it is a pity that the paving was not made a little wider. Every now and then we met one of the huge, unwieldy carts which seem to be relics of a prehistoric age—rough plank affairs of enormous strength and a design so primitive as to be a constant source of wonder. They could only be pulled along at a slow walk and with vast effort by a couple of huge horses, and the load the cart was carrying never seemed to bear any proportion to the mechanism of its transport. The roads are bad, but they will not account for those carts. The little front wheels are a stroke of mechanical ineptitude positively amounting to genius, and when they are replaced by a single wheel, and the whole affair resembles a huge tricycle, one instinctively looks round for a Dinosaur. Time after time we met them stuck in the mud or partially overturned, but the drivers seemed in no way disconcerted; it was evidently all part of the regular business of the day. When one thinks of the Brussels coachwork which adorns our most expensive motors, and of the great engineering works of Liège, those carts are a really wonderful example of persistence of type.

We passed through Bruges at a pace positively disrespectful to that fine old town. There is no town in Belgium so uniform in the magnificence of its antiquity, and it is good to think that—so far, at any rate—it has escaped destruction. As we crossed the square, the clock in the belfry struck the hour, and began to play its chimes. It is a wonderful old clock, and every quarter of an hour it plays a tune—a very attractive performance, unless you happen to live opposite. I remember once thinking very hard things about the maker of that clock, but perhaps it was not his fault that one of the bells was a quarter of a tone flat. At the gates our passports were examined, and we travelled on to Ghent by the Ecloo Road, one of the main thoroughfares of Belgium. Beyond an occasional sentry, there was nothing to indicate that we were passing through a country at war, except that we rarely saw a man of military age. All were women, old men, or children. Certainly the men of Belgium had risen to the occasion. The women were doing everything—working in the fields, tending the cattle, driving the market-carts and the milk-carts with their polished brass cans. After leaving Ghent, the men came into view, for at Lokeren and St. Nicholas were important military stations, whilst nearer to Antwerp very extensive entrenchments and wire entanglements were being constructed. The trenches were most elaborate, carefully constructed and covered in; and I believe that all the main approaches to the city were defended in the same way. Antwerp could never have been taken by assault, but with modern artillery it would have been quite easy to destroy it over the heads of its defenders. The Germans have probably by now rendered it impregnable, for though in modern war it is impossible to defend one's own cities, the same does not apply to the enemy. In future, forts will presumably be placed at points of strategic importance only, and as far as possible from towns.

Passing through the western fortifications, we came upon the long bridge of boats which had been thrown across the Scheldt. The river is here more than a quarter of a mile wide, and the long row of sailing barges was most picturesque. The roadway was of wooden planks, and only just wide enough to allow one vehicle to pass at a time, the tall spars of the barges rising on each side. It is strange that a city of such wealth as Antwerp should not have bridged a river which, after all, is not wider than the Thames. We were told that a tunnel was in contemplation. The bridge of boats was only a tribute to the necessities of war. We did not dream that a fortnight later it would be our one hope of escape.

II

THE HOSPITAL

ANTWERP is one of the richest cities in Europe, and our hospital was placed in its wealthiest quarter. The Boulevard Leopold is a magnificent avenue, with a wide roadway in the centre flanked by broad paths planted with trees. Beyond these, again, on each side is a paved road with a tram-line, whilst a wide pavement runs along the houses. There are many such boulevards in Antwerp, and they give to the city an air of spaciousness and opulence in striking contrast to the more utilitarian plan of London or of most of our large towns. We talk a great deal about fresh air, but we are not always ready to pay for it.

Our hospital occupied one of the largest houses on the south-east side. A huge doorway led into an outer hall through which the garden was directly reached behind the house. On the right-hand side of this outer hall a wide flight of steps led to inner glass doors and the great central hall of the building. As a private house it must have been magnificent; as a hospital it was as spacious and airy as one could desire. The hall was paved with marble, and on either side opened lofty reception rooms, whilst in front wide marble staircases led to the first floor. This first floor and another above it were occupied entirely by wards, each containing from six to twelve beds. On the ground floor on the right-hand side were two large wards, really magnificent rooms, and one smaller, all these overlooking the Boulevard. On the left were the office, the common room, and the operating theatre. Behind the house was a large paved courtyard, flanked on the right by a garden border and on the left by a wide glass-roofed corridor. The house had previously been used as a school, and on the opposite side of the courtyard was the gymnasium, with dormitories above. The gymnasium furnished our dining-hall, whilst several of the staff slept in the rooms above.

It will be seen that the building was in many ways well adapted to the needs of a hospital and to the accommodation of the large staff required. We had in all 150 beds, and a staff of about 50. The latter included 8 doctors, 20 nurses, 5 dressers, lay assistants, and motor drivers. In addition to these there was a kitchen staff of Belgians, so that the management of the whole was quite a large undertaking, especially in a town where ordinary provisions were becoming more and more

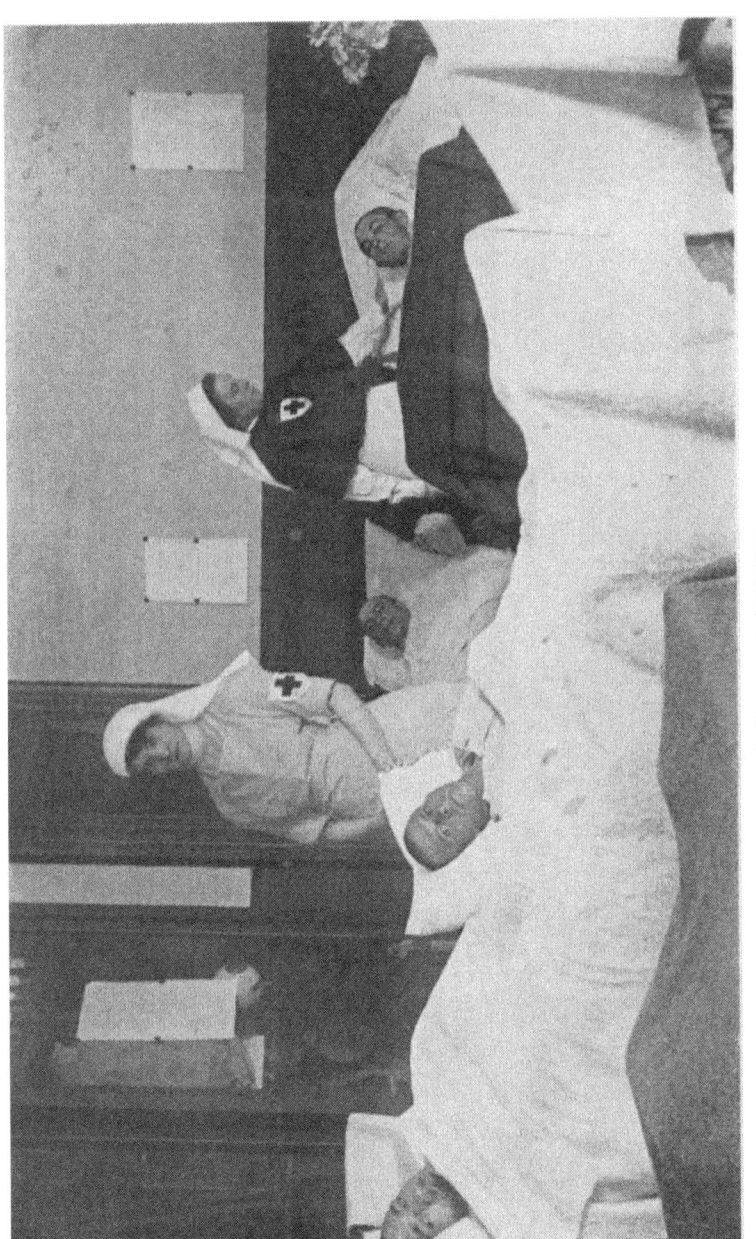

A Ward at Antwerp.

THE HOSPITAL

difficult to obtain. In the later days of the siege, when milk was not to be had and the only available water was salt, the lot of our housekeeper was anything but happy. Providing meals for over 200 people in a besieged town is no small matter. But it was managed somehow, and our cuisine was positively astonishing, to which I think we largely owe the fact that none of the staff was ever ill. Soldiers are not the only people who fight on their stomachs.

The management of the hospital centred in the office, and it was so typical of Belgium as to be really worth a few words of description. It was quite a small room, and it was always crowded. Four of us had seats round a table in the centre, and at another table in the window sat our Belgian secretary, Monsieur Herman, and his two clerks. But that was only the beginning of it. All day long there was a constant stream of men, women, and children pouring into that room, bringing letters, asking questions, always talking volubly to us and amongst themselves. At first we thought that this extraordinary turmoil was due to our want of space, but we soon found that it was one of the institutions of the country. In England an official's room is the very home of silence, and is by no means easy of access. If he is a high official, a series of ante-rooms is interposed between his sacred person and an inquisitive world. But in Belgium everyone walks straight in without removing his cigar. The great man sits at his desk surrounded by a perfect Babel, but he is always polite, always ready to hear what you have to say and to do what he can to help. He appears to be able to deal with half a dozen different problems at the same time without ever being ruffled or confused. There is an immense amount of talking and shaking of hands, and at first the brain of a mere Englishman is apt to whirl; but the business is done rapidly and completely. Belgium is above all things democratic, and our office was a good introduction to it.

The common room was large and airy, overlooking the courtyard, and a few rugs and armchairs made it a very comfortable place when the work of the day was done. Anyone who has worked in a hospital will know what a difference such a room makes to the work—work that must be carried on at all hours of the day or night; nor will he need to be told of the constant supply of tea and coffee that will be found there. We go about telling our patients of the evils of excessive tea-drinking, and we set them an example they would find it hard to follow. We do not mention how often tea and a hot bath have been our substitute for a night's sleep. A good common room

THE HOSPITAL 15

and an unlimited supply of tea will do much to oil the wheels of hospital life.

But to myself the all-important room was the operating theatre, for upon its resources depended entirely our opportunities for surgical work. It was in every way admirable, and I know plenty of hospitals in London whose theatres would not bear comparison with ours. Three long windows faced the courtyard; there was a great bunch of electric lights in the ceiling, and there was a constant supply of boiling water. What more could the heart of surgeon desire? There were two operating tables and an equipment of instruments to vie with any in a London hospital. Somebody must have been very extravagant over those instruments, I thought as I looked at them; but he was right and I was wrong, for there were very few of those instruments for which I was not grateful before long. The surgery of war is a very different thing from the surgery of home.

The wards were full when we arrived, and I had a wonderful opportunity of studying the effects of rifle and shell fire. Most of the wounds were fortunately slight, but some of them were terrible, and, indeed, in some cases it seemed little short of miraculous that the men had survived. But on every side one saw nothing but cheerful faces, and one would never have dreamt what some of those men had gone through. They were all smoking cigarettes, laughing, and chatting, as cheery a set of fellows as one could meet. You would never have suspected that a few days before those same men had been carried into the hospital in most cases at their last gasp from loss of blood and exposure, for none but serious cases were admitted. The cheeriest man in the place was De Rasquinet, a wounded officer who had been christened " Ragtime " for short, and for affection. A week before he had been struck by a shell in the left side, and a large piece of the shell had gone clean through, wounding the kidney behind and the bowel in front. That man crawled across several fields, a distance of nearly a mile, on his hands and knees, dragging with him to a place of safety a wounded companion. When from loss of blood he could drag him along no longer, he left him under a hedge, and dragged himself another half-mile till he could get help. When he was brought into the hospital, he was so exhausted from pain and loss of blood that no one thought that he could live for more than a few hours, but by sheer pluck he had pulled through. Even now he was desperately ill with as horrible a wound as a man could have, but nothing was going to depress him. I am glad to say that what is known in surgery as a short circuit was an immediate success, and when

THE HOSPITAL

we left him three weeks later in Ghent he was to all intents perfectly well.

There were plenty of other serious cases, some of them with ghastly injuries, and many of them must have suffered agonizing pain; but they were all doing their best to make light of their troubles, whilst their gratitude for what was done for them was extraordinary. The Belgians are by nature a cheerful race, but these were brave men, and we felt glad that we had come out to do what we could for them.

But if we give them credit for their courage and cheerfulness, we must not forget how largely they owed it to the devoted attention—yes, and to the courage and cheerfulness—of the nurses. I wonder how many of us realize what Britain owes to her nurses. We take them as a matter of course, we regard nursing as a very suitable profession for a woman to take up—if she can find nothing better to do; perhaps we may have been ill, and we were grateful for a nurse's kindness. But how many of us realize all the long years of drudgery that have given the skill we appreciated, the devotion to her work that has made the British nurse what she is? And how many of us realize that we English-speaking nations alone in the world have such nurses? Except in small groups, they are unknown in France, Belgium, Germany,

Russia, or any other country in the world. In no other land will women leave homes of ease and often of luxury to do work that no servant would touch, for wages that no servant would take—work for which there will be very little reward but the unmeasured gratitude of the very few. They stand to-day as an unanswerable proof that as nations we have risen higher in the level of civilization than any of our neighbours. To their influence on medicine and surgery I shall refer again. Here I only wish to acknowledge our debt. As a mere patient I would rather have a good nurse than a good physician, if I were so unfortunate as to have to make the choice. A surgeon is a dangerous fellow, and must be treated with respect. But as a rule the physician gives his blessing, the surgeon does his operation, but it is the nurse who does the work.

THE DAY'S WORK

IN any hospital at home or abroad there is a large amount of routine work, which must be carried on in an orderly and systematic manner, and upon the thoroughness with which this is done will largely depend the effectiveness of the hospital. Patients must be fed and washed, beds must be made and the wards swept and tidied, wounds must be dressed and splints adjusted. In an English hospital everything is arranged to facilitate this routine work. Close to every ward is a sink-room with an adequate supply of hot and cold water, dinner arrives in hot tins from the kitchens as if by magic, whilst each ward has its own arrangements for preparing the smaller meals. The beds are of a convenient height, and there is an ample supply of sheets and pillow-cases, and of dressing materials of all kinds arranged on tables which run noiselessly up and down the wards. At home all these things are a matter of course; abroad they simply did not exist. Four or five gas-rings represented our hot-water supply and our ward-kitchens for our 150 patients, and the dinners had to be carried up from the large kitchens in the basement. The beds were so low as to break one's back, and had iron sides which were always in the way; and when we came to the end of our sheets—well, we came to the end of them, and that was all. In every way the work was heavier and more difficult than at home, for all our patients were heavy men, and every wound was septic, and had, in many cases, to be dressed several times a day. Everyone had to work hard, sometimes very hard; but as a rule we got through the drudgery in the morning, and in the afternoon everything was in order, and we should, I think, have compared very favourably in appearance with most hospitals at home.

But we had to meet one set of conditions which would, I think, baffle many hospitals at home. Every now and then, without any warning, from 50 to 100, even in one case 150, wounded would be brought to our door. There was no use in putting up a notice "House Full"; the men were wounded and they must be attended to. In such a case our arrangement was a simple one: all who could walk went straight upstairs, the gravest cases went straight to the theatre or waited their turn in the great hall, the others were accommodated on the ground floor. We had a number

THE DAY'S WORK 21

of folding beds for emergency, and we had no rules as to overcrowding. In the morning the authorities would clear out as many patients as we wished. Sometimes we were hard put to it to find room for them all, but we always managed somehow, and we never refused admission to a single patient on the score of want of room. The authorities soon discovered the capacity of the hospital for dealing with really serious cases, and as a result our beds were crowded with injuries of the gravest kind. What appealed to us far more was the appreciation of the men themselves. We felt that we had not worked in vain when we heard that the soldiers in the trenches begged to be taken " à l'Hôpital Anglais."

The condition of the men when they reached us was often pitiable in the extreme. Most of them had been living in the trenches for weeks exposed to all kinds of weather, their clothes were often sodden and caked with dirt, and the men themselves showed clear traces of exposure and insecure sleep. In most cases they had lain in the trenches for hours after being wounded, for as a rule it is impossible to remove the wounded at once with any degree of safety. Indeed, when the fighting is at all severe they must lie till dark before it is safe for the stretcher-bearers to go for them. This was so at Furnes, but at Antwerp we were usually able to get them in within a few hours. Even a few hours' delay with a bad wound may be a serious matter, and in every serious case our attention was first directed to the condition of the patient himself and not to his wound. Probably he had lost blood, his injury had produced more or less shock, he had certainly been lying for hours in pain. He had to be got warm, his circulation had to be restored, he had to be saved from pain and protected from further shock. Hot bottles, blankets, brandy, and morphia worked wonders in a very short time, and one could then proceed to deal with wounds. Our patients were young and vigorous, and their rate of recovery was extraordinary.

When a rush came we all had to work our hardest, and the scenes in any part of the hospital required steady nerves; but perhaps the centre of interest was the theatre. Here all the worst cases were brought—men with ghastly injuries from which the most hardened might well turn away in horror; men almost dead from loss of blood, or, worst of all, with a tiny puncture in the wall of the abdomen which looks so innocent, but which, in this war at least, means, apart from a difficult and dangerous operation, a terrible death. With all these we had to deal as rapidly and completely as possible, reducing each case to

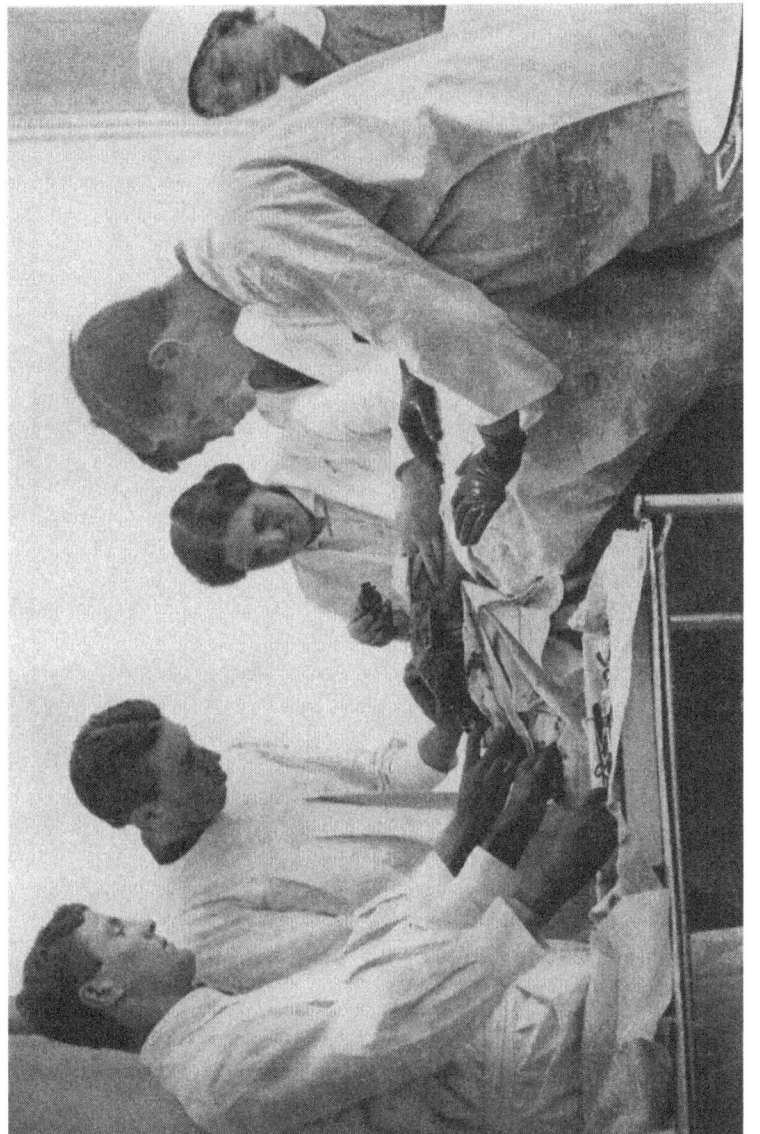

An Operation at Antwerp.

Underwood phot.

a form which it would be practicable to nurse, where the patient would be free from unnecessary pain, and where he would have the greatest possible chance of ultimate recovery. Of course, all this was done under anæsthesia. What a field hospital must have been before the days of anæsthesia is too horrible to contemplate. Even in civil hospitals the surgeons must have reached a degree of "Kultur" beside which its present exponents are mere children. It is not so many years since a famous surgeon, who was fond of walking back from his work at the London Hospital along the Whitechapel Road, used to be pointed to with horror by the Aldgate butchers, whose opinion on such a subject was probably worth consideration. But now all that is changed. The surgeon can be a human being again, and indeed, except when he goes round his wards, his patients may never know of his existence. They go to sleep in a quiet ante-room, and they waken up in the ward. Of the operation and all its difficulties they know no more than their friends at home. Perhaps even more wonderful is the newer method of spinal anæsthesia, which we used largely for the difficult abdominal cases. With the injection of a minute quantity of fluid into the spine all sensation disappears up to the level of the arms, and, provided he cannot see what is going on, any operation below that level can be carried out without the patient knowing anything about it at all. It is rather uncanny at first to see a patient lying smoking a cigarette and reading the paper whilst on the other side of a screen a big operation is in progress. But for many cases this method is unsuitable, and without chloroform we should indeed have been at a loss. The Belgians are an abstemious race, and they took it beautifully. I am afraid they were a striking contrast to their brothers on this side of the water. Chloroform does not mix well with alcohol in the human body, and the British working man is rather fond of demonstrating the fact.

With surgery on rather bold lines it was extraordinary how much could be done, especially in the way of saving limbs. During the whole of our stay in Antwerp we never once had to resort to an amputation. We were dealing with healthy and vigorous men, and once they had got over the shock of injury they had wonderful powers of recovery. We very soon found that we were dealing with cases to which the ordinary rules of surgery did not apply. The fundamental principles of the art must always be the same, but here the conditions of their application were essentially different from those of civil practice. Two of

THE DAY'S WORK

these conditions were of general interest: the great destruction of the tissues in most wounds, and the infection of the wounds, which was almost universal.

Where a wound has been produced by a large fragment of shell, one expects to see considerable damage; in fact, a whole limb may be torn off, or death may be instant from some terrible injury to the body. But where the object of the enemy is the injury of individuals, and not the destruction of buildings, they often use shrapnel, and the resulting wounds resemble those from the old smooth-bore guns of our ancestors. Shrapnel consists of a large number of bullets about half an inch in diameter packed together in a case, which carries also a charge of explosive timed to burst at the moment when it reaches its object. The balls are small and round, and if they go straight through soft tissues they do not do much damage. If, however, they strike a bone, they are so soft that their shape becomes irregular, and the injury they can produce in their further course is almost without limit. On the whole, they do not as a rule produce great damage, for in many cases they are nearly spent when they reach their mark. Pieces of the case will, of course, have much the same effect as an ordinary shell.

The effects of rifle-fire, particularly at short

ranges, have led to a great deal of discussion, and each side has accused the other of using dumdum bullets. The ordinary bullet consists of a lead core with a casing of nickel, since the soft lead would soon choke rifling. Such a bullet under ordinary circumstances makes a clean perforation, piercing the soft tissues, and sometimes the bones, with very little damage. In a dumdum bullet the casing at the tip is cut or removed, with the result that, on striking, the casing spreads out and forms a rough, irregular missile, which does terrific damage. Such bullets were forbidden by the Geneva Convention. But the German bullet is much more subtle than this. It is short and pointed, and when it strikes it turns completely over and goes through backwards. The base of the bullet has no cover, and consequently spreads in a manner precisely similar to that in a dum-dum, with equally deadly results. There could be no greater contrast than that between the wounds with which we had to deal in South Africa, produced by ordinary bullets, and those which our soldiers are now receiving from German rifles. The former were often so slight that it was quite a common occurrence for a soldier to discover accidentally that he had been wounded some time previously. In the present war rifle wounds have been amongst the most deadly with which we have had to deal.

It will thus be seen that in most cases the wounds were anything but clean-cut; with very few exceptions, they were never surgically clean. By surgically clean we mean that no bacteria are present which can interfere with the healing of the tissues, and only those who are familiar with surgical work can realize the importance of this condition. Its maintenance is implied in the term "aseptic surgery," and upon this depends the whole distinction between the surgery of the present and the surgery of the past. Without it the great advances of modern surgery would be entirely impossible. When we say, then, that every wound with which we had to deal was infected with bacteria, it will be realized how different were the problems which we had to face compared with those of work at home. But the difference was even more striking, for the bacteria which had infected the wounds were not those commonly met with in England. These wounds were for the most part received in the open country, and they were soiled by earth, manure, fragments of cloth covered with mud. They were therefore infected by the organisms which flourish on such soil, and not by the far more deadly denizens of our great cities. It is true that in soil one may meet with tetanus and other virulent bacteria, but in our experience these were rare. Now, there is one way in which all such infections may be defeated—by plenty of fresh air, or, better still, by oxygen. We had some very striking proofs of this, for in several cases the wounds were so horribly foul that it was impossible to tolerate their presence in the wards; and in these cases we made it a practice to put the patient in the open air, of course suitably protected, and to leave the wound exposed to the winds of heaven, with only a thin piece of gauze to protect it. The results were almost magical, for in two or three days the wounds lost their odour and began to look clean, whilst the patients lost all signs of the poisoning which had been so marked before. It may be partly to this that we owe the fact that we never had a case of tetanus. In all cases we treated our wounds with solutions of oxygen, and we avoided covering them up with heavy dressings; and we found that this plan was successful as well as economical.

Though any detailed description of surgical treatment would be out of place, there was one which in these surroundings was novel, and which was perhaps of general interest. Amongst all the cases which came to us, certainly the most awkward were the fractured thighs. It was not a

THE DAY'S WORK

question of a broken leg in the ordinary sense of the term. In every case there was a large infected wound to deal with, and as a rule several inches of the bone had been blown clean away. At first we regarded these cases with horror, for anything more hopeless than a thigh with 6 inches missing it is difficult to imagine. Splints presented almost insuperable difficulties, for the wounds had to be dressed two or three times, and however skilfully the splint was arranged, the least movement meant for the patient unendurable agony. After some hesitation we attempted the method of fixation by means of steel plates, which was introduced with such success by Sir Arbuthnot Lane in the case of simple fractures. The missing portion of the bone is replaced by a long steel plate, screwed by means of small steel screws to the portions which remain, "demonstrating," as a colleague put it, "the triumph of mind over the absence of matter." The result was a brilliant success, for not only could the limb now be handled as if there were no fracture at all, to the infinite comfort of the patient, but the wounds themselves cleared up with great rapidity. We were told that the plates would break loose, that the screws would come out, that the patient would come to a bad end through the violent sepsis induced by the presence of a "foreign body" in the shape of the steel plate. But none of these disasters happened, the cases did extremely well, and one of our most indignant critics returned to his own hospital after seeing them with his pockets full of plates. The only difficulty with some of them was to induce them to stop in bed, and it is a fact that on the night of our bombardment I met one of them walking downstairs, leaning on a dresser's arm, ten days after the operation.

And this brings me to a subject on which I feel very strongly, the folly of removing bullets. If a bullet is doing any harm, pressing on some nerve, interfering with a joint, or in any way causing pain or inconvenience, by all means let it be removed, though even then it should in most cases never be touched until the wound is completely healed. But the mere presence of a bullet inside the body will of itself do no harm at all. The old idea that it will cause infection died long ago. It may have brought infection with it; but the removal of the bullet will not remove the infection, but rather in most cases make it fire up. We now know that, provided they are clean, we can introduce steel plates, silver wires, silver nets, into the body without causing any trouble at all, and a bullet is no worse than any of these. It is a matter in which the public are very largely to blame, for they consider that unless the bullet has been removed the surgeon has not done his job. Unless he has some specific reason for it, I know that the surgeon who removes a bullet does not know his work. It may be the mark of a Scotch ancestry, but if I ever get a bullet in my own anatomy, I shall keep it.

IV

ANTWERP

THERE is no port in Europe which holds such a dominant position as Antwerp, and there is none whose history has involved such amazing changes of fortune. In the middle of the sixteenth century she was the foremost city in Europe, at its close she was ruined. For two hundred years she lay prostrate under the blighting influence of Spain and Austria, and throttled by the commercial jealousy of England and Holland. A few weeks ago she was the foremost port on the Continent, the third in the world; now her wharves stand idle, and she herself is a prisoner in the hands of the enemy. Who can tell what the next turn of the wheel will bring?

Placed centrally between north and south, on a deep and wide river, Antwerp is the natural outlet of Central Europe towards the West, and it is no wonder that four hundred years ago she gathered to herself the commerce of the Netherlands, in which Ypres, Bruges, and Ghent had been her forerunners. For fifty years she was the Queen

ANTWERP

of the North, and the centre of a vast ocean trade with England, France, Spain, Portugal, and Italy, till the religious bigotry of Philip II. of Spain and the awful scenes of the Spanish Fury reduced her to ruin. For two hundred years the Scheldt was blocked by Holland, and the ocean trade of Antwerp obliterated. Her population disappeared, her wharves rotted, and her canals were choked with mud. It is hard to apportion the share of wickedness between a monarch who destroys men and women to satisfy his own religious lust, and a nation which drains the life-blood of another to satisfy its lust for gold. One wonders in what category the instigator of the present war should appear.

At the very beginning of last century Napoleon visited Antwerp, and asserted that it was "little better than a heap of ruins." He recognized its incomparable position as a port and as a fortress, and he determined to raise it to its former prosperity, and to make it the strongest fortress in Europe. He spent large sums of money upon it, and his refusal to part with Antwerp is said to have broken off the negotiations of Chatillon, and to have been the chief cause of his exile to St. Helena. Alas! his enemies did not profit by his genius. We are the allies of his armies now, but we have lost Antwerp. Germany will be utterly and completely crushed before she parts with that incomparable prize. A mere glance at the map of Europe is sufficient to convince anyone that in a war between England and Germany it is a point of the first strategical importance. That our access to it should be hampered by the control of Holland over the Scheldt is one of the eccentricities of diplomacy which are unintelligible to the plain man. The blame for its loss must rest equally between Britain and Belgium, for Belgium, the richest country in Europe for her size, attempted to defend her greatest stronghold with obsolete guns; whilst we, who claim the mastery of the seas, sacrificed the greatest seaport in Europe to the arrangements of an obsolete diplomacy. If we are to retain our great position on the seas, Antwerp must be regained. She is the European outpost of Britain, and, as has so often been pointed out, the mouth of the Scheldt is opposite to the mouth of the Thames.

In Antwerp, as we saw her, it was almost impossible to realize the vicissitudes through which she had passed, or to remember that her present prosperity was of little more than fifty years' growth. On all sides we were surrounded by wide boulevards, lined by magnificent houses and public buildings. There are few streets in Europe to eclipse the great Avenue des Arts, which, with its continuations, extends the whole length of the city from north to south. The theatres, the Central Station, the banks, would adorn any city, and the shops everywhere spoke of a wealth not restricted to the few. The wide streets, the trees, the roomy white houses, many of them great palaces, made a deep impression upon us after the darkness and dirt of London. Even in the poorer quarters there was plenty of light and air, and on no occasion did we find the slums which surround the wealthiest streets all over London. In the older parts of the city the streets were, of course, narrower; but even here one had the compensation of wonderful bits of architecture at unexpected corners, splendid relics of an illustrious past. They are only remnants, but they speak of a time when men worked for love rather than for wages, and when an artisan took a pride in the labour of his hands. If it had not been for the hand of the destroyer, what a marvellous city Antwerp would have been! One likes to think that the great creations of the past are not all lost, and that in the land to which the souls of the Masters have passed we may find still living the mighty thoughts to which their love gave birth. Are our cathedrals only stones and mortar, and are our paintings only dust and oil?

The inhabitants of Antwerp were as delightful as their city. On all sides we were welcomed with a kindness and a consideration not always accorded to those who are so bold as to wish to help their fellow-men. Everywhere we met with a courtesy and a generosity by which, in the tragedy of their country, we were deeply touched. They all seemed genuinely delighted to see us, from the Queen herself to the children in the streets. Our medical confrères treated us royally, and the mere thought of professional jealousy with such men is simply ludicrous. They constantly visited our hospital, and they always showed the keenest interest in our work and in any novelties in treatment we were able to show them; and when we went to see them, we were shown all the best that they had, and we brought away many an ingenious idea which it was worth while going far to obtain. Wherever we moved amongst the Belgians, we always found the same simplicity of purpose, the same generosity of impulse. Everywhere we met the same gratitude for what England was doing for Belgium; no one ever referred to the sacrifices which Belgium has made for England.

The one thing which so impressed us in the character of the Belgians whom we met was its simplicity, and the men who had risen to high

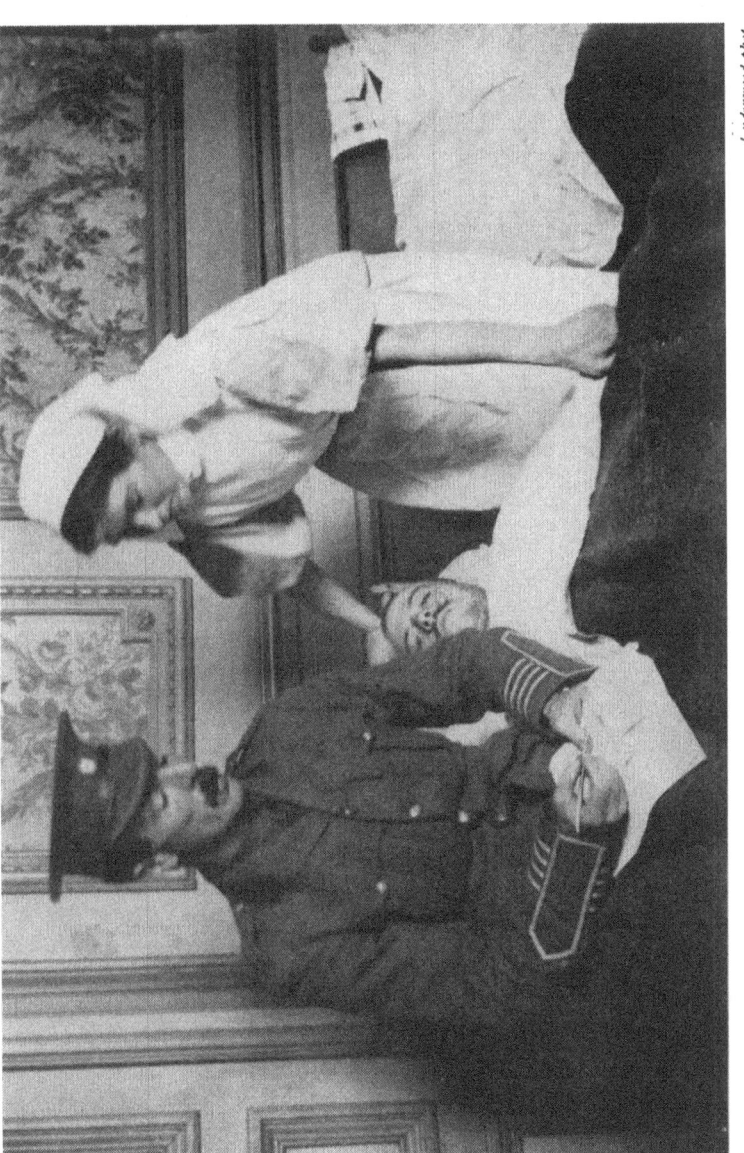

THE DIRECTOR, DR. BEAVIS, AT ANTWERP.

rank did not seem to have lost it in their climb to fame. But it was just this, the most delightful of their characteristics, which must have made war for them supremely difficult. For strict discipline and simplicity are almost incompatible. None of us tower so far above our fellows that we can command instant obedience for our own sakes. We have to cover ourselves with gold lace, to entrench ourselves in rank, and to provide ourselves with all sorts of artificial aids before we can rely on being obeyed. These things are foreign to the Belgian mind, and as a result one noticed in their soldiers a certain lack of the stern discipline which war demands. Individually they are brave men and magnificent fighters. They only lacked the organization which has made the little British Army the envy of the world. The fact is that they are in no sense a warlike nation, in spite of their turbulent history of the past, and, indeed, few things could be more incompatible than turbulence and modern warfare. It demands on the part of the masses of combatants an obedience and a disregard of life which are repellent to human nature, and the Belgians are above all things human. Germany is governed by soldiers, and France by officials. Unlike the frogs in the fable, the Belgians are content to govern themselves.

It was our great regret that we had so little time in which to see the work of the Antwerp hospitals, but we made use of what opportunities we had. There are many of them, and those we saw were magnificent buildings, equipped in a way which filled us with envy. The great city hospital, the Stuivenberg, was a model of what a modern hospital ought to be. The wards were large and airy and spotlessly clean, and the nurses seemed to be extremely competent. The kitchens were equipped with all the latest appliances, steam boilers, and gas and electric cookers. But the show part of the hospital was the suite of operating theatres. I have always felt the pardonable pride of a son in the theatres of the London Hospital, but they were certainly eclipsed here. Each theatre was equipped with its own anæsthetizing room, its own surgeon's room, and its own sterilizing rooms and stores, all furnished with a lavishness beyond the financial capacity of any hospital in London. Perhaps some of the equipment was unnecessary, but it was abundantly evident that the State appreciated the value of first-class surgery, and that it was prepared to pay for it. I have never heard the same accusation levelled at Great Britain.

At St. Camille we had the good fortune to see M. Lambotte at work. His reputation as a surgeon is worldwide, and it was pleasant to find that his dexterity as an operator was equal to his reputation. It is not always the case. He is an expert mechanic, and himself makes most of the very ingenious instruments which he uses. He was fixing a fractured femur with silver wires, and one could see the skilled workman in all that he did. There is no training-ground for one's hands like a carpenter's bench, and the embryo surgeon might do much worse with his time than spend six months of it in a workshop. When medical training emerges from its medieval traditions, manual training will certainly form a part, and no one will be allowed to attempt to mend a bone till he has shown his capacity to mend a chair-leg. Here, again, the surgeon was surrounded by all the appliances, and even the luxuries, that he could desire. The lot of the great surgeon abroad is indeed a happy one.

But there is one thing in which we in England are far better off—in our nursing staffs. In most of the hospitals we visited the nursing was carried on by Sisterhoods, and though some of them were evidently good nurses, most of them had no idea whatever of nursing as it is practised in our country. Fresh air, for example, is to them full of dangers. One would almost think that it savoured of the powers of evil. We went into one huge hospital of the most modern type, and equipped lavishly, and such was the atmosphere that in ten minutes I had to make a rush for the door. One large ward was full of wounded soldiers, many of them with terrible wounds, gangrenous and horrible, and every window was tightly shut. How they could live in such an atmosphere is beyond my comprehension, but the Sisters did not seem to notice it at all.

Some of the surgeons have their specially trained nurses, but nursing as a profession for the classes who are alone competent to undertake it is a conception which has yet to dawn upon the Continent, for only a woman of education and refinement can really be a nurse.

The absence on the Continent of a nursing profession such as ours is not without its influence on medicine and surgery abroad. The individual patient meets with far less consideration than would be the case in this country, and is apt to be regarded as so much raw material. In Belgium this tendency is counteracted by the natural kindliness of the Belgian, but in other countries patients are often treated with a callousness which is amazing. There is in many of the great clinics a disregard of the patient's feelings, of his sufferings, and even of his life, which would be impossible in an English hospital. The contact of a surgeon with his hospital patients as individuals is largely through the nursing staff, and his point of view will be largely influenced by them. There is no one in our profession, from the youngest dresser to the oldest physician, who does not owe a great part of his education to Sister.

V
TERMONDE

ANYONE who has worked in hospitals will realize how important it is for the health of the staff, nurses and doctors, that they should get out into the fresh air for at least some part of every day. It is still more necessary in a war hospital, for not only is the work more exacting, but the cases themselves involve certain risks which can only be safely taken in perfect health. Practically every one is septic, and to anyone in the least run down the danger of infection is considerable; and infection with some of the organisms with which one meets in war is a very serious thing indeed. We had four large motors in Antwerp belonging to the members of our hospital, and always at its service, and every afternoon parties were made up to drive out into the country. As a rule calls were made at various Croix Rouge posts on the way, and in that way we kept in contact with the medical service of the army in the field, and gave them what help we could. We were always provided with the password, and the whole country

TERMONDE 43

was open to us—a privilege we very greatly appreciated; for after a hard morning's work in the wards there are few things more delightful than a motor drive. And it gave us an opportunity of seeing war as very few but staff officers ever can see it. We learnt more about the condition of the country and of the results of German methods in one afternoon than all the literature in the world could ever teach. If only it were possible to bring home to the people of Britain one-hundredth part of what we saw with our own eyes, stringent laws would have to be passed to stop men and women from enlisting. No man who deserved the name of man, and no woman who deserved to be the mother of a child, would rest day or night till the earth had been freed from the fiends who have ravaged Belgium and made the name of German vile.

One afternoon towards the end of September we visited Termonde. We heard that the Germans, having burnt the town, had retired, leaving it in the hands of the Belgian troops. It was a rare opportunity to see the handiwork of the enemy at close quarters, and we did not wish to miss it. Termonde is about twenty-two miles from Antwerp, and a powerful car made short work of the distance. Starting directly southwards through Boom, we reached Willebroeck and the road which runs east and west from Malines through Termonde to Ghent, and along it we turned to the right. We were now running parallel to the German lines, which at some points were only a couple of miles away on the other side of the Termonde-Malines railway. We passed numerous Belgian outposts along the road, and for a few miles between Lippeloo and Baesrode they begged us to travel as fast as possible, as at this point we came within a mile of the railway. We did travel, and it would have taken a smart marksman to hit us at fifty miles an hour; but we felt much happier when we passed under the railway bridge of a loop line at Briel and placed it between ourselves and the enemy. The entrance to Termonde was blocked by a rough barricade of bricks and branches guarded by a squad of soldiers. They told us that no one was allowed to pass, and we were about to return disappointed, when one of us happened to mention the password. As without it we could not possibly have got so far, it had never occurred to us that they might think we had not got it; and as we had no possible business in the town, we had no arguments to oppose to their refusal to let us in. However, all was now open to us, and the cheery fellows ran forward to remove the barrier they had put up.

Termonde is, or rather was, a well-to-do town

TERMONDE

of 10,000 inhabitants lying on the Scheldt at the point where the Dendre, coming up from the south, runs into it. A river in Belgium means a route for traffic, and the town must have derived some advantage from its position as a trade junction. But it possesses an even greater one in the bridge which here crosses the Scheldt, the first road bridge above the mouth of the river, for there is none at Antwerp. At least six main roads converge upon this bridge, and they must have brought a great deal of traffic through the town. When we mention that a corresponding number of railways meet at the same spot, it will be seen that Termonde was an important centre, and that it must have been a wealthy town. The Dendre runs right through the centre of the town to the point where it joins the Scheldt, and on each side runs a long stone quay planted with trees, with old-fashioned houses facing the river. With the little wooden bridges and the barges on the river it must have been a very pretty picture. Now it was little better than a heap of ruins.

The destruction of the town was extraordinarily complete, and evidently carefully organized. The whole thing had been arranged beforehand at headquarters, and these particular troops supplied with special incendiary apparatus. There is strong evidence to show that the destruction of

Louvain, Termonde, and of several smaller towns, was all part of a definite plan of "frightfulness," the real object being to terrorize Holland and Denmark, and to prevent any possibility of their joining with the Allies. It is strictly scientific warfare, it produces a strictly scientific hell upon this world, and I think that one may have every reasonable hope that it leads to a strictly scientific hell in the next. After a town has been shelled, its occupants driven out, and its buildings to a large extent broken down, the soldiers enter, each provided with a number of incendiary bombs, filled with a very inflammable compound. They set light to these and throw them into the houses, and in a very few minutes each house is blazing. In half an hour the town is a roaring furnace, and by the next day nothing is left but the bare walls. And that is almost all that there was left of Termonde. We walked along the quay beside a row of charred and blackened ruins, a twisted iron bedstead or a battered lamp being all there was to tell of the homes which these had been. A few houses were still standing untouched, and on the door of each of these was scrawled in chalk the inscription:

"Gute Leute,
"Nicht Anzünden,
"Breitfuss, *Lt.*"

TERMONDE.

Underwood phot.

One wondered at what cost the approval of Lieutenant Breitfuss had been obtained. His request to the soldiers not to set fire to the houses of these " good people " had been respected, but I think that if the Belgians ever return to Termonde those houses are likely to be empty. There are things worse than having your house burnt down, and one would be to win the approval of Lieutenant Breitfuss.

We crossed the Dendre and wandered up the town towards the Square. For a few moments I stood alone in a long curving street with not a soul in sight, and the utter desolation of the whole thing made me shiver. Houses, shops, banks, churches, all gutted by the flames and destroyed. The smell of burning from the smouldering ruins was sickening. Every now and then the silence was broken by the fall of bricks or plaster. Except a very few houses with that ominous inscription on their doors, there was nothing left; everything was destroyed. A little farther on I went into the remains of a large factory equipped with elaborate machinery, but so complete was the destruction that I could not discover what had been made there. There was a large gas engine and extensive shafting, all hanging in dismal chaos, and I recognized the remains of machines for making tin boxes, in which the products of the factory had,

I suppose, been packed. A large pile of glass stoppers in one corner was fused up into a solid mass, and I chipped a bit off as a memento.

In the Square in front of the church of Notre Dame the German soldiers had evidently celebrated their achievement by a revel. In the centre were the remains of a bonfire, and all around were broken bottles and packs of cheap cards in confusion. Think of the scene. A blazing town around them, and every now and then the crash of falling buildings; behind them Notre Dame in flames towering up to heaven; the ancient Town Hall and the Guard House burning across the Square; and in the centre a crowd of drunken soldiers round a bonfire, playing cards. And miles away across the fields ten thousand homeless wanderers watching the destruction of all for which they had spent their lives in toil.

Of the ancient church of Notre Dame only the walls remained. The roof had fallen, all the woodwork had perished in the flames, and the stonework was calcined by the heat. Above the arch of a door was a little row of angels' heads carved in stone, but when we touched them they fell to powder. The heat inside must have been terrific, for all the features of the church had disappeared, and we were surrounded by merely a mass of débris. In the apse a few fragments of old gold

TERMONDE

brocade buried beneath masses of brick and mortar were all that remained to show where the altar had been.

The Town Hall was once a beautiful gabled building with a tall square tower ending in four little turrets. I have a drawing of it, and it must have formed quite a pleasing picture, the entrance reached by the double flight of steps of which Belgium is so fond, and from which public proclamations were read. It had been only recently restored, and it was now to all intents and purposes a heap of smoking bricks. The upper part of the tower had fallen into the roof, and the whole place was burnt out.

But no words can ever convey any idea of the utter destruction of the whole town, or of the awful loneliness by which one was surrounded. One felt that one was in the presence of wickedness such as the world has rarely seen, that the powers of darkness were very near, and that behind those blackened walls there lurked evil forms. Twilight was coming on as we turned back to our car, and a cold mist was slowly rising from the river. I am not superstitious, and in broad daylight I will scoff at ghosts with anyone, but I should not care to spend a night alone in Termonde. One could almost hear the Devil laughing at the handiwork of his children.

VI
THE CHÂTEAU

ONE of the most astounding features of the war is the way in which the Germans, from the highest to the lowest, have given themselves up to loot. In all previous wars between civilized countries anything in the nature of loot has been checked with a stern hand, and there are cases on record when a soldier has been shot for stealing a pair of boots. But now the Crown Prince of the German Empire sends back to his palaces all the loot that he can collect, on innumerable transport waggons, amid the applause of his proud father's subjects. He is of course carrying out the new gospel of the Fatherland that everyone has a perfect right to whatever he is strong enough to take. But some day that doctrine may spread from the exalted and sacred circle in which it is now the guiding star to the "cannon fodder." Some day the common people will have learnt the lesson which is being so sedulously taught to them both by example and by precept, and then the day of reckoning will have come.

THE CHÂTEAU 51

Loot and destruction have always gone hand in hand. The private soldier cannot carry loot, and it is one of the most primitive instincts of animal nature to destroy rather than to leave that by which others may profit. Even the pavement artist will destroy his work rather than allow some poor wretch to sit beside his pictures and collect an alms. And there is great joy in destroying that which men are too coarse to appreciate, in feeling that they have in their power that which, something tells them, belongs to a refinement they cannot attain. That was the keynote of the excesses of the French Revolution, for nothing arouses the fury of the unclean so much as cleanliness, and a man has been killed before now for daring to wash his hands. And it is this elemental love of destroying that has raged through Belgium in the last few months, for though destruction has been the policy of their commanders, the German soldier has done it for love. No order could ever comprehend the ingenious detail of much that we saw, for it bore at every turn the marks of individuality. It is interesting to ponder on a future Germany of which these men, or rather these wild beasts, will be the sons. Germany has destroyed more than the cities of Belgium; she has destroyed her own soul.

It is not in the ruined towns or the battered

cathedrals of Belgium that one sees most clearly the wholehearted way in which the German soldiers have carried out the commands of their lord and made his desires their own. Louvain, Termonde, Dinant, and a hundred other towns have been uprooted by order. If you wish to see what the German soldier can do for love, you have to visit the châteaux which are dotted so thickly all over the Belgian countryside. Here he has had a free hand, and the destruction he wrought had no political object and served no mere utilitarian purpose. It was the work of pure affection, and it showed Germany at her best. One would like to have brought one of those châteaux over to England, to be kept for all time as an example of German culture, that our children might turn from it in horror, and that our country might be saved from the hypocrisy and the selfishness of which this is the fruit.

Among our many good friends in Antwerp there were few whom we valued more than the Baron d'O. He was always ready to undertake any service for us, from the most difficult to the most trivial. A man of birth and of fortune, he stood high in the service of the Belgian Government, and he was often able to do much to facilitate our arrangements with them. So when he asked us to take him out in one of our cars to see

THE CHÂTEAU

the château of one of his greatest friends, we were glad to be in a position to repay him in a small way for his kindness. The château had been occupied by the Germans, who had now retired—though only temporarily, alas!—and he was anxious to see what damage had been done and to make arrangements for putting it in order again if it should be possible.

A perfect autumn afternoon found us tearing southwards on the road to Boom in Mrs. W.'s powerful Minerva. We were going to a point rather close to the German lines, and our safety might depend on a fast car and a cool hand on the wheel. We had both, for though the hand was a lady's, its owner had earned the reputation of being the most dangerous and the safest driver in Antwerp, and that is no mean achievement. We called, as was our custom, at the Croix Rouge stations we passed, and at one of them we were told that there were some wounded in Termonde, and that, as the Germans were attacking it, they were in great danger. So we turned off to the right, and jolted for the next twenty minutes over a deplorable paved road.

The roar of artillery fire gradually grew louder and louder, and we were soon watching an interesting little duel between the forts of Termonde, under whose shelter we were creeping along, on the one side, and the Germans on the other. The latter were endeavouring to destroy one of the bridges which span the Scheldt at this point, one for the railway and one for the road; but so far they had not succeeded in hitting either. It was a week since our last visit to Termonde, and it seemed even more desolate and forsaken than before. The Germans had shelled it again, and most of the remaining walls had been knocked down, so that the streets were blocked at many points and the whole town was little more than a heap of bricks and mortar. There was not a living creature to be seen, and even the birds had gone. The only sound that broke the utter silence was the shriek of the shells and the crash of their explosion. We were constantly checked by piles of fallen débris, and from one street we had to back the car out and go round by another way. At the end of a long street of ruined houses, many bearing the inscription of some braggart, " I did this," we found our wounded men. They were in a monastery near the bridge at which the Germans were directing their shells, several of which had already fallen into the building. There had been four wounded men there, but two of them, badly hurt, were so terrified at the bombardment that they had crawled away in the night. The priest thought that they were prob-

THE CHÂTEAU 55

ably dead. Think of the poor wounded wretches, unable to stand, crawling away in the darkness to find some spot where they could die in peace. Two remained, and these we took with us on the car. The priest and the two nuns, the sole occupants of the monastery, absolutely refused to leave. They wished to protect the monastery from sacrilege, and in that cause they held their lives of small account. I have often thought of those gentle nuns and the fearless priest standing in the doorway as our car moved away. I hope that it went well with them, and that they did not stay at their post in vain.

By the bridge stood a company of Belgian soldiers, on guard in case, under cover of the fire of their artillery, the Germans might attempt to capture it. There was very little shelter for them, and it was positively raining shells; but they had been told to hold the bridge, and they did so until there was no longer a bridge to hold. It was as fine a piece of quiet heroism as I shall ever see, and it was typical of the Belgian soldier wherever we saw him. They never made any fuss about it, they were always quiet and self-contained, and always cheerful. But if they were given a position to hold, they held it. And that is the secret of the wonderful losing battle they have fought across Belgium. Some day they will advance and not retreat, and then I think that the Belgian Army will astonish their opponents, and perhaps their friends too.

We were soon out of Termonde and on the open road again, to our very great relief, and at the nearest dressing-station we handed over our patients, who were not badly wounded, to the surgeon, who was hard at work in a little cottage about a mile back along the road. We drove on due east, and forty minutes later found ourselves at the entrance of the lodge of our friend's house. It lay on the very edge of the Belgian front, and would have been unapproachable had there been any activity in this section of the line. Fortunately for us, the Germans were concentrating their energies around Termonde, and the mitrailleuse standing on the path amongst the trees at the end of the garden seemed to have gone asleep.

We turned the car in the drive, and, in case things should happen, pointed its nose homewards. That is always a wise precaution, for turning a car under fire in a narrow road is one of the most trying experiences imaginable. The coolest hand may fumble with the gears at such a moment, and it is surprising how difficult it is to work them neatly when every second may be a matter of life or death, when a stopped engine may settle the fate of everyone in the car. It is foolish to take unnecessary risks, and we left the car pointing the right way, with its engine running, ready to start on the instant, while we went to have a look at the house.

It was a large country-house standing in well-timbered grounds, evidently the home of a man of wealth and taste. The front-door stood wide open, as if inviting us to enter, and as we passed into the large hall I could not help glancing at our friend's face to see what he was thinking as the obvious destruction met us on the very threshold. So thorough was it that it was impossible to believe that it had not been carried out under definite orders. Chairs, sofas, settees lay scattered about in every conceivable attitude, and in every case as far as I can recollect minus legs and backs. In a small room at the end of the hall a table had been overturned, and on the floor and around lay broken glass, crockery, knives and forks, mixed up in utter confusion, while the wall was freely splashed with ink. One fact was very striking and very suggestive: none of the pictures had been defaced, and there were many fine oil-paintings and engravings hanging on the walls of the reception-rooms. After the destruction of the treasures of Louvain, it is absurd to imagine that the controlling motive could have been any reverence for works of art. The explanation was obvious enough. The pictures were of value, and were the loot of some superior officer. A large cabinet had evidently been smashed with the butt-end of a musket, but the beautiful china it contained was intact. The grand piano stood uninjured, presumably because it afforded entertainment. The floor was thick with playing cards.

But it was upstairs that real chaos reigned. Every wardrobe and receptacle had been burst open and the contents dragged out. Piles of dresses and clothing of every kind lay heaped upon the floor, many of them torn, as though the harsh note produced by the mere act of tearing appealed to the passion for destruction which seemed to animate these fighting men. In the housekeeper's room a sewing-machine stood on the table, its needle threaded, and a strip of cloth in position, waiting for the stitch it was destined never to receive. There were many other things to which one cannot refer, but it would have been better to have had one's house occupied by a crowd of wild beasts than by these apostles of culture.

Our friend had said very little while we walked through the deserted rooms in this splendid country-house in which he had so often stayed. Inside the house he could not speak, and it was not until we got out into the sunshine that he could relieve his overwrought feelings. Deep and bitter

THE CHÂTEAU

were the curses which he poured upon those vandals; but I stood beside him, and I did not hear half that he said, for my eyes were fixed on the mitrailleuse standing on the garden path under the trees. My fingers itched to pull the lever and to scatter withering death among them. It slowly came into my mind how good it would be to kill these defilers. I suppose that somewhere deep down in us there remains an elemental lust for blood, and though in the protected lives we live it rarely sees the light, when the bonds of civilization are broken it rises up and dominates. And who shall say that it is not right ? There are things in Belgium for which blood alone can atone. Woe to us if when our interests are satisfied we sheath the sword, and forget the ruined homes, the murdered children of Belgium, the desecrated altars of the God in whose name we fight ! He has placed the sword in our hands for vengeance, and not for peace.

I no longer wonder at the dogged courage of the Belgian soldiers, at their steady disregard of their lives, when I think of the many such pictures of wanton outrage which are burned into their memories, and which can never be effaced so long as a single German remains in their beloved land. I no longer wonder, but I do not cease to admire. Let anyone who from the depths of an armchair at home thinks that I have spoken too strongly, stimulate his imagination to the pitch of visualizing the town in which he lives destroyed, his own house a smoking heap, his wife profaned, his children murdered, and himself ruined, for these are the things of which we know. Then, and then only, will he be able to judge the bravery of the nation which, preferring death to dishonour, has in all likelihood saved both France and ourselves from sharing its terrible but glorious fate.

VII

MALINES

WE were frequently requested by the Belgian doctors to assist them in the various Red Cross dressing-stations around Antwerp, and it was our custom to visit several of these stations each day to give what assistance we could. One of the most important of the stations was at Malines, and one of our cars called there every day. I went out there myself on an afternoon late in September. It was a glorious day, and after a heavy morning in the wards the fresh breeze and the brilliant sunshine were delightful. Our road led almost straight south through Vieux Dieu and Contich, crossing the little River Nethe at Waelhem. The Nethe encircles Antwerp on the south and south-east, and it was here that the Belgians, and in the end the British, made their chief stand against the Germans. We crossed the bridge, and passed on to Malines under the guns of Fort Waelhem, with the great fortress of Wavre St. Catharine standing away to the left, impregnable to anything but the huge guns of to-day.

Malines is a large town of 60,000 inhabitants, and is the cathedral city of the Archbishop of Belgium, the brave Cardinal Mercier. To-day it is important as a railway centre, and for its extensive railway workshops, but the interest of the town lies in the past. It was of importance as early as the eighth century, and since then it has changed hands on an amazing number of occasions. Yet it is said that few of the cities of Europe contain so many fine old houses in such good preservation. The cathedral church of St. Rombold dates back to the thirteenth century, and in the fifteenth century was begun the huge tower which can be seen for many miles around. It was intended that it should be 550 feet high—the highest in the world—and though it has reached little more than half that height, it is a very conspicuous landmark. The Germans evidently found it a very tempting mark, for they began shelling it at an early stage. When we were there the tower had not been damaged, but a large hole in the roof of the church showed where a shell had entered. Inside everything was in chaos. Every window was broken, and of the fine stained glass hardly a fragment was left. A large portion of the roof was destroyed, and the floor was a confusion of chairs and débris. The wonderful carved wooden pulpit, with its almost life-size figures, was

MALINES 63

damaged. When the shell entered, the preacher's notes from the previous Sunday lay on the desk, and they were perforated by a fragment.

The Croix Rouge was established in a large school on the south side of the town. We drove into the large courtyard, and went in to see if there was anything for us to do. The doctor in charge, a distinguished oculist, was an old friend and was very cordial, but he said there was no fighting near, and that no cases had come in. We stood talking for a few minutes, and were just going, when one of our other cars came in with a man very badly wounded. He was a cyclist scout, and had been shot while crossing a field a few miles away. He had been picked up at considerable risk by our people—for the Germans rarely respected a Red Cross—and brought in on the ambulance. He was wounded in the abdomen, and his right arm was shattered. He was in a desperate state, but the doctor begged me to do what I could for him, and, indeed, the power of recovery of these fellows was so remarkable that it was always worth a trial. As rapidly as possible we got ready stimulants and hot saline solution to inject into his veins. We had not come prepared for actual operating, and the local equipment was meagre, but we succeeded in improvising a transfusion apparatus out of various odds and ends. It did not take long to get it to work, and in a few minutes he began to respond to the hot salt and water running into his vessels. Alas! it was only for a moment. He was bleeding internally, and nothing could be done. I went over to the priest, who had just come, and said: "C'est à vous, monsieur." He bowed, and came forward holding in his hands the holy oil. A few murmured words were spoken, the priest's finger traced the sign of the Cross, a few moments of silence, and all was over. Death is always impressive, but I shall never forget that scene. The large schoolroom, with its improvised equipment, ourselves, a crowd of nurses and doctors standing round, in the centre the sandalled priest bending downwards in his brown mantle, and the dying man, his lips moving to frame the last words he would speak on earth. It was in silence that we stole out into the sunlight of the courtyard.

We went on to Sempst, a small village at the extreme limit of the Belgian lines. A little stream ran under the road beside a farm, and a rough breastwork had been thrown across the road to defend the bridge. German soldiers could be seen a mile down the road moving behind the trees. It was only a small Belgian outpost, but it was a good enough position to hold, so long as the enemy did not bring up artillery. A machine gun was hidden beside the bridge, and would have made short work of anyone advancing up the road. My friends were talking to the men, whom we knew quite well, and for a moment I was standing alone, when one of the soldiers came up and asked about the man whom we had just left, and who had come from near by. I told him what had happened, and for a moment he did not speak. At last he looked up at me with tears in his eyes, and said simply: " He was my brother, and this morning we were laughing together." I held his hand for a moment, and then he turned away and went back to his post.

Our way home led past a villa where an encounter had taken place three days before between the Belgians and an advanced detachment of German troops, and we stopped to see the scene of the fighting. It was a large country-house standing back in its own grounds, and during the night a party of Germans had succeeded in concealing themselves inside. In the morning, by a ruse, they induced a Belgian detachment to come up the drive towards the house, never suspecting that it was not empty. Suddenly the Germans opened fire, and I believe that scarcely a single Belgian escaped. Next day, however, having surrounded the villa, the Belgians opened fire upon it with their 3-inch guns. The

Germans made a bolt for it, and the whole of them were killed. As we walked up the drive we saw on the left-hand side a little row of graves with fresh flowers laid on them. They were the graves of the Belgian soldiers who had been entrapped. An officer was standing by them with bared head, and, seeing us, he came over and walked on with us to the house, which he was then occupying with his soldiers. It was a fine house, with polished parquet floors and wide staircases. The dining-room was ornamented with delicate frescoes in gilt frames. In the drawing-room stood a new grand pianoforte, and light gilt chairs and sofas, looking strangely out of place on the field of war. By the front-door, sticking in the wall, was a shell which had failed to burst. I wonder if it is still there, or if anyone has ventured to shift it. It was half inside and half outside, and if it had exploded there would not have been much of the entrance of the house left. Upstairs the rooms were in glorious confusion. Apparently the Germans had opened all the drawers, and flung their contents on the floor, with the idea, I suppose, of taking anything they wanted. One room was plainly the nursery, for the floor was covered with children's toys of all descriptions, all broken. It may be very unreasonable, but that room made me more angry than all the rest of the house. There is something so utterly wanton in trampling on a child's toys. They may be of no value, but I have a small opinion of a man who does not treat them with respect. They are the symbols of an innocence that once was ours, the tokens of a contact with the unseen world for which we in our blindness grope longingly in vain.

VIII

LIERRE

WHEN, years hence, some historian looks back upon the present war, and from the confusion of its battles tries to frame before his mind a picture of the whole, one grim conclusion will be forced upon his mind. He will note, perhaps, vast alterations in the map of Europe; he will lament a loss of life such as only the hand of Heaven has dealt before; he will point to the folly of the wealth destroyed. But beneath all these he will hear one insistent note from which he cannot escape, the deep keynote of the whole, the note on which the war was based, the secret of its ghastly chords, and the foundation of its dark conclusion. And he will write that in the year 1914 one of the great nations of civilized Europe relapsed into barbarism.

In the large sense a nation becomes civilized as its members recognize the advantages of sinking their personal desires and gain in the general good of the State. The fact that an individual can read and write and play the piano has nothing at all to do with the degree of his civilization, an elementary axiom of which some of our rulers seem strangely ignorant. To be of use to the State, and to train others to be of use to the State (and not only of use to themselves), should be, and indeed *is*, the aim of every truly civilized man. Unless it be so, his civilization is a mere veneer, ready to wear off at the first rub, and he himself a parasite upon the civilized world.

As time has gone on, the State has laid down certain rules by means of which the men who formed it could serve it better, and these are our laws which we obey not for our own good directly, but for the good of the State. From the point of view of the plain man in the street, it is all utterly illogical, for it would be logical to go and take from your neighbour whatever you wished, so long as you were strong enough to hold it. But, let us thank Heaven, no sane man is logical, and only a Professor would dare to make the claim. It is one of the prerogatives of his office, and should be treated with tolerance.

And as our views of life are small and limited by our surroundings, when States grew large they took from the shoulders of the individual his responsibilities in the great State which the world has now become; and the States of which the world was composed agreed together on certain rules which should control their relations to one another, not for the good of each, but for the good of the greater State of which they were members. They are not so accurately laid down as the laws of our separate States, but they are broad, general principles for the use of statesmen and not of legalists. They are the Charter of Civilization among the nations of the world, and the nation which disregards them does so at her peril, and has handed in the abnegation of her position as a civilized State. Like the laws of each State, they are utterly illogical—at least, to those who have made up their minds that they are strong enough to hold what they can take from their neighbours.

I am often told, in half-defence of what they have done, that the Germans are conducting the war in a strictly logical manner. At first, I must admit, I was rather taken with the idea, and, indeed, one felt almost sorry for a noble nation sacrificing its feelings on the uncompromising altar of Logic. For the object of war is obviously to defeat your enemy, and it may be argued that anything which will accelerate that result is not only justifiable, but almost humane, for it will shorten the unavoidable horrors of war. I should like to mention a few of the features of logical warfare, all of which have at one time or another been adopted by our opponents, and I shall then describe as far as I can an example which I myself saw.

When an army wishes to pass through a country, the civil population is in the way. To get rid of them, the best plan, and the quickest, is to annihilate the first town of a suitable size to which the army comes. If the town is wiped out, and men, women, and children slaughtered indiscriminately, it will make such an impression in the rest of the country that the whole population will clear out and there will be no further trouble. The country will then be free for the passage of troops, and there will be no troublesome civil population to feed or govern. The conduct of the war will be greatly facilitated. Of course, it will be necessary at intervals to repeat the process, but this presents the further advantage that it advertises to other nations what they may expect if war enters their borders. This, one of the most elementary rules of logical warfare, has been strictly observed by Germany. The sack of Louvain and the slaughter of its inhabitants met with an immediate success. Wherever the German army arrived, they entered with few exceptions empty towns. Termonde, Malines, Antwerp, had everything swept and garnished for their reception. It would, of course, be absurdly illogical to confine one's attack to persons capable of defence. To kill a hundred women and children makes far more impression than to kill a thousand men, and it is far safer, unless, of course, it is preferred to use them as a screen to protect your own advancing troops from the enemy's fire.

It is a mistake to burden your transport with the enemy's wounded, or, indeed—low be it spoken—with your own. The former should always be killed, and the latter so far as the degree of culture of your country will allow. It is one of the regrettable points, logically, of Germany's warfare that she appears to pay some attention to her wounded, but our information on this point is deficient, and it is possible that she limits it to those who may again be useful.

To kill the Medical Staff of the enemy is obviously most desirable. Without them a large number of the wounded would die. If, therefore, it is possible to kill both the doctors and the wounded together, it is a great advantage, and of all possible objectives for artillery a hospital is the most valuable. So complete was our confidence in the German observance of this rule that when we heard that they were likely to bombard Antwerp, we were strongly advised to remove our Red Cross from the sight of prying aeroplanes, and we took the advice. Several other hospitals were hit, but we escaped.

There are many other rules of logical warfare, such as ignoring treaties, engagements, and, indeed, the truth in any form. But these are those with which I myself came in contact, and which therefore interested me the most. There is only one unfortunate objection to logical warfare, and that is that it is the duty of the whole civilized world, as it values its eternal salvation, to blot out from the face of the earth they have defiled the nation which practises it.

I do not wish to be unfair to those with whom we are fighting, or to arouse against them an unjust resentment. I am merely attempting to express succinctly the doctrines which have been proclaimed throughout Germany for years, of which this war is the logical outcome, and in the light of which alone its incidents can be understood. She is the home of logic, the temple where material progress is worshipped as a god. For her there is no meaning in those dim yearnings of the human mind, in which logic has no part, since their foundations are hidden in depths beneath our ken, but which alone separate us from the beasts that perish. And, above all things, I would not be thought to include in such a sweeping statement all those who call themselves German. There are many in Germany who are not of this Germany, and in the end it may be for them as much as for ourselves that we shall have fought this war.

It is only when viewed in this setting that a scene such as that we saw at Lierre can be understood. By itself it would stand naked, meaningless, and merely horrible. Clothed in these 'thoughts, it is pregnant with meaning, and forms a real epitome of the whole German conception of war; for horror is their dearest ally, and that scene has left on my mind a feeling of horror which I do not think that time will ever eradicate.

Lierre is an old-world town on the River Nethe, nine miles south of Antwerp, prosperous, and thoroughly Flemish. Its 20,000 inhabitants weave silk and brew beer, as they did when London was a village. Without the physical advantages of Antwerp, and without the turbulence of Ghent, Lierre has escaped their strange vicissitudes, and for hundreds of years has enjoyed the prosperity of a quiet and industrious town. Its church of St. Gommarius is renowned for its magnificent proportions, its superb window tracery, and its wonderful rood-loft—features in which it has eclipsed in glory even the great cathedrals of Belgium, and which place it alone as a unique

LIERRE.

Underwood phot.

achievement of the art of the fifteenth century. It is in no sense a military town, and has no defences, though there is a fort of the same name at no great distance from it.

Into this town, without warning of any kind, the Germans one morning dropped two of their largest shells. One fell near the church, but fortunately did no harm. One fell in the Hospital of St. Elizabeth. We heard in Antwerp that several people had been wounded, and in the afternoon two of us went out in one of our cars to see if we could be of any service. We found the town in the greatest excitement, and the streets crowded with families preparing to leave, for they rightly regarded these shells as the prelude of others. In the square was drawn up a large body of recruits just called up—rather late in the day, it seemed to us. We slowly made our way through the crowds, and, turning to the right along the Malines road, we drew up in front of the hospital on our right-hand side. The shell had fallen almost vertically on to a large wing, and as we walked across the garden we could see that all the windows had been broken, and that most of the roof had been blown off. The nuns met us, and took us down into the cellars to see the patients. It was an infirmary, and crowded together in those cellars lay a strange medley of people. There were bedridden old women huddled up on mattresses, almost dead with terror. Wounded soldiers lay propped up against the walls; and women and little children, wounded in the fighting around, lay on straw and sacking. Apparently it is not enough to wound women and children; it is even necessary to destroy the harbour of refuge into which they have crept. The nuns were doing for them everything that was possible, under conditions of indescribable difficulty. They may not be trained nurses, but in the records of this war the names of the nuns of Belgium ought to be written in gold. Utterly careless of their own lives, absolutely without fear, they have cared for the sick, the wounded, and the dying, and they have faced any hardship and any danger rather than abandon those who turned to them for help.

The nuns led us upstairs to the wards where the shell had burst. The dead had been removed, but the scene that morning must have been horrible beyond description. In the upper ward six wounded soldiers had been killed, and in the lower two old women. As we stood in the upper ward, it was difficult to believe that so much damage could have been caused by a single shell. It had struck almost vertically on the tiled roof, and, exploding in the attic, had blown in the ceiling into the upper ward. I had not realized before that the explosion of a large shell is not absolutely instantaneous, but, in consequence of the speed of the shell, is spread over a certain distance. Here the shell had continued to explode as it passed down through the building, blowing the floor of the upper ward down into the ward below. A great oak beam, a foot square, was cut clean in two, the walls of both wards were pitted and pierced by fragments, and the tiled floor of the lower ward was broken up. The beds lay as they were when the dead were taken from them, the mattresses riddled with fragments and soaked with blood. Obviously no living thing could have survived in that awful hail. When the shell came the soldiers were eating walnuts, and on the bed of one lay a walnut half opened and the little penknife he was using, and both were stained. We turned away sickened at the sight, and retraced the passage with the nuns. As we walked along, they pointed out to us marks we had not noticed before—red finger-marks and splashes of blood on the pale blue distemper of the wall. All down the passage and the staircase we could trace them, and even in the hall below. Four men had been standing in the doorway of the upper ward. Two were killed; the others, bleeding and blinded by the explosion, had groped their way along that wall and down the stair. I have seen many terrible sights, but for utter and concentrated horror I have never seen anything to equal those finger-marks, the very sign-manual of Death. When I think of them, I see, in the dim light of the early autumn morning, the four men talking; I hear the wild shriek of the shell and the deafening crash of its explosion; and then silence, and two bleeding men groping in darkness and terror for the air.

IX

A PAUSE

THE life of a hospital at the front is a curious mixture of excitement and dulness. One week cases will be pouring in, the operating theatre will be working day and night, and everyone will have to do their utmost to keep abreast of the rush; next week there will be nothing to do, and everyone will mope about the building, and wonder why they were ever so foolish as to embark on such a futile undertaking. For it is all emergency work, and there is none of the dull routine of the ordinary hospital waiting list, which we are always trying to clear off, but which is in reality the backbone of the hospital's work.

When we first started in Antwerp, the rush of cases was so great as to be positively overwhelming. For more than twenty-four hours the surgeons in the theatre were doing double work, two tables being kept going at the same time. During that time a hundred and fifty wounded were admitted, all of them serious cases, and the hospital was full to overflowing. For the next ten days we were kept busy, but then our patients began to recover, and many of them had to go away to military convalescent hospitals. The wards began to look deserted, and yet no more patients arrived. We began to think that it was all a mistake that we had come, that there would be no more fighting round Antwerp, and that we were not wanted. Indeed, we canvassed the possibilities of work in other directions, and in the meantime we drew up elaborate arrangements to occupy our time. There were to be courses of lectures and demonstrations in the wards, and supplies of books and papers were to be obtained. Alas! for the vanity of human schemes, the wounded began to pour in again, and not a lecture was given.

During that slack week we took the opportunity to see a certain amount of Antwerp, and to call on many officials and the many friends who did so much to make our work there a success and our stay a pleasure. To one lady we can never be sufficiently grateful. She placed at our disposal her magnificent house, a perfect palace in the finest quarter of the city. Several of our nurses lived there, we had a standing invitation to dinner, and, what we valued still more, there were five bathrooms ready for our use at any hour of the day. Their drawing-room had been converted into a ward for wounded officers, and held

A PAUSE

about twenty beds. One of the daughters had trained as a nurse, and under her charge it was being run in thoroughly up-to-date style. The superb tapestries with which the walls were decorated had been covered with linen, and but for the gilded panelling it might have been a ward in a particularly finished hospital. I often wonder what has happened to that house. The family had to fly to England, and unless it was destroyed by the shells, it is occupied by the Germans.

Calling in Antwerp on our professional brethren was very delightful for one's mind, but not a little trying for one's body. Their ideas of entertainment were so lavish, and it was so difficult to refuse their generosity, that it was a decided mistake to attempt two calls in the same afternoon. To be greeted at one house with claret of a rare vintage, and at the next with sweet champagne, especially when it is plain that your host will be deeply pained if a drop is left, is rather trying to a tea-drinking Briton. They were very good to us, and we owed a great deal to their help. Most of all we owed to Dr. Morlet, for he had taken radiographs of all our fractures, and of many others of our cases. We went to see him one Sunday afternoon at his beautiful house in the Avenue Plantin. He also had partly converted his house into a hospital for the wounded, and we saw twenty or thirty of them in a large drawing-room. The rest of the house was given up to the most magnificent electro-therapeutical equipment I have ever seen or heard of. We wandered through room after room filled with superb apparatus for X-ray examinations, X-ray treatment, diathermy, and electrical treatment of every known kind. It was not merely that apparatus for all these methods was there. Whole rooms full of apparatus were given up to each subject. It was the home of a genius and an enthusiast, who thought no sum too great if it were to advance his science. Little did we think that ten days later we should pick its owner up upon the road from Antwerp, a homeless wanderer, struggling along with his wife and his family, leaving behind everything he possessed in the world, in the hope that he might save them from the Germans. We heard from him not long ago that they had carried off to Germany all the wonderful machinery on which he had spent his life.

The very next morning, while we were still at breakfast, the wounded began to arrive, and we never had another day in Antwerp that was not crowded with incident. The wounded almost always came in large batches, and the reason of this was the method of distribution adopted by the authorities. All the injured out at the front

A PAUSE

were collected as far as possible to one centre, where a train was waiting to receive them. There they remained until the train was sufficiently filled, when it brought them into the Central Station of Antwerp. At this point was established the distributing station, with a staff of medical officers, who arranged the destination of each man. Antwerp has a very complete system of electric trams, scarcely a street being without one, and of these full use was made for the transport of the wounded. Those who could sit went in ordinary cars, but for the stretcher cases there were cars specially fitted to take ordinary stretchers. A car was filled up with cases for one hospital, and in most cases it could deposit them at the door. It was an admirable method of dealing with them, simple and expeditious, and it involved far less pain and injury to the men than a long journey on an ambulance. In fact, we were only allowed in exceptional circumstances to bring in wounded on our cars, and it is obvious that it was a wise plan, for endless confusion would have been the result if anyone could have picked up the wounded and carried them off where they liked. Our cars were limited for the most part to carrying the injured to the various dressing-stations and to the train, and for these purposes they were always welcomed. They were soon well known at the trenches, and wherever the fighting was heaviest you might be sure to find one of them. Many were the hairbreadth escapes of which they had to tell, for if there were wounded they brought them out of danger, shells or no shells. And it says as much for the coolness of the drivers as for their good luck that no one was ever injured; for danger is halved by cool judgment, and a bold driver will come safely through where timidity would fail.

X

THE SIEGE

It is difficult to say exactly when the Siege of Antwerp began. For weeks we heard the distant boom of the guns steadily drawing nearer day by day, and all night the sky was lit up by distant flashes. But so peculiar was the position of Antwerp that it was not till the last ten days that our life was seriously affected, and not till the very end that communication with our friends and the getting of supplies became difficult. Our first real domestic tragedy was the destruction of the waterworks on the 30th of September. They lay just behind Waelhem, some six miles south of Antwerp, and into them the Germans poured from the other side of Malines a stream of 28-centimetre shells, with the result that the great reservoir burst. Until one has had to do without a water-supply in a large city it is impossible to realize to what a degree we are dependent upon it. In Antwerp, fortunately, a water-supply has been regarded as somewhat of an innovation, and almost every house, in the better class quarters at least, has its own wells and pumps. It was, however, the end of the summer, and the wells were low; our own pumps would give us barely enough water for drinking purposes. The authorities did all they could, and pumped up water from the Scheldt for a few hours each day, enabling us, with considerable difficulty, to keep the drainage system clear. But this water was tidal and brackish, whilst as to the number of bacteria it contained it was better not to inquire. We boiled and drank it when we could get nothing else, but of all the nauseous draughts I have ever consumed, not excluding certain hospital mixtures of high repute, tea made with really salt water is the worst. Coffee was a little better, though not much, and upon that we chiefly relied. But I really think that that was one of the most unpleasant of our experiences. A more serious matter from the point of view of our work was the absence of water in the operating theatre. We stored it as well as we could in jugs, but in a rush that was inadequate, and we began to realize what the difficulties were with which surgeons had to contend in South Africa. We were really driven out of Antwerp at a very fortunate moment, and I have often wondered what we should have done if we had stopped there for another week.

Such a very large proportion of the inhabitants

THE SIEGE

of Antwerp had already disappeared that there was never any great shortage of supplies. Milk and butter were the first things to go, and fresh vegetables followed soon after. It was always a mystery to me that with the country in such a condition they went on for as long as they did. The peasants must have worked their farms until they were absolutely driven out, and indeed in our expeditions into the country we often saw fields being ploughed and cattle being fed when shells were falling only a few fields away. However, margarine and condensed milk are not bad substitutes for the real articles, and the supply of bread held out to the very end. A greater difficulty was with our kitchen staff of Belgian women, for a good many of them took fright and left us, and it was not at all easy to get their places filled.

As the week went on the pressure of the enemy became steadily greater. On Tuesday, the 29th of September, the great fortress of Wavre St. Catherine fell, blown up, it is believed, by the accidental explosion of a shell inside the galleries. It had been seriously battered by the big German howitzers, and it could not in any case have held out for another day. But the results of the explosion were terrible. Many of the wounded came to us, and they were the worst cases we had so far seen. On Thursday Fort Waelhem succumbed after a magnificent resistance. The garrison held it until it was a mere heap of ruins, and, indeed, they had the greatest difficulty in making their way out. I think that there is very little doubt that the Germans were using against these forts their largest guns, the great 42-centimetre howitzers. It is known that two of these were brought northwards past Brussels after the fall of Maubeuge, and a fragment which was given to us was almost conclusive. It was brought to us one morning as an offering by a grateful patient, and it came from the neighbourhood of Fort Waelhem. It was a mass of polished steel two feet long, a foot wide, and three inches thick, and it weighed about fifty pounds. It was very irregular in shape, with edges sharp as razors, without a particle of rust upon it. It had been picked up where it fell still hot, and it was by far the finest fragment of shell I have ever seen. Alas! we had to leave it behind, and it lies buried in a back-garden beside our hospital. Some day it will be dug up, and will be exhibited as conclusive evidence that the Germans did use their big guns in shelling the town. The destruction produced by such a shell is almost past belief. I have seen a large house struck by a single shell of a much smaller size than this, and it simply crumpled up like a pack of cards. As a house it disappeared, and all that

THE SIEGE

was left was a heap of bricks and mortar. When one considers that these guns have a range of some ten miles, giving Mont Blanc considerable clearance on the way, and that one of them out at Harrow could drop shells neatly into Charing Cross, some idea of their power can be obtained.

Every day we had visits from the enemy's aeroplanes, dropping bombs or literature, or merely giving the range of hospitals and other suitable objectives to the German gunners. From the roof of the hospital one could get a magnificent view of their evolutions, and a few kindred spirits always made a rush for a door on to the roof, the secret of which was carefully preserved, as the accommodation was limited. It was a very pretty sight to watch the Taube soaring overhead, followed by the puffs of smoke from the explosion of shells fired from the forts. The puffs would come nearer and nearer as the gunners found the range, until one felt that the next must bring the Taube down. Then suddenly the airman would turn his machine off in another direction, and the shells would fall wider than ever. One's feelings were torn between admiration for the airman's daring and an unholy desire to see him fall.

It was evident that Antwerp could not withstand much longer the pressure of the enemy's guns, and we were not surprised when on Friday we received an official notice from the British Consul-General, Sir Cecil Herstlet, that the Government were about to leave for Ostend, and advising all British subjects to leave by a boat which had been provided for them on Saturday. On Saturday morning came an order from the Belgian Army Medical Service instructing us to place on tramcars all our wounded, and to send them to the railway station. It appeared evident that Antwerp was to be evacuated, and we took the order to clear out our wounded as an intimation that our services would be no longer required. We got all our men ready for transport, and proceeded to pack up the hospital. The tramcars arrived, and we bade good-bye to our patients, and saw them off, some in ordinary trams and some in specially equipped stretcher-cars. It was a dismal scene.

The hall of the hospital was still covered with stretchers on which lay patients waiting their turn for the cars to take them, and the whole hospital was in process of being dismantled, when tramcars began to arrive back from the station with the patients we had just packed off. They told us that the whole of Antwerp was covered with tramloads of wounded soldiers, that there were five thousand in the square in front of the railway station, and that two trains had been

THE SIEGE

provided to take them away! It was evident that some extraordinary blunder had been made; and while we were in doubt as to what to do, a second order came to us cancelling entirely the evacuation order which we and all the other hospitals in Antwerp had received a few hours before. It was all so perplexing that we felt that the only satisfactory plan was to go round to the British Consul and find out what it all meant. We came back with the great news that British Marines were coming to hold Antwerp. That was good enough for us. In less than an hour the hospital was in working order again, and the patients were back in their beds, and a more jubilant set of patients I have never seen. It was the most joyful day in the history of the hospital, and if we had had a case of champagne, it should have been opened. As it was, we had to be content with salt coffee.

But there was one dreadful tragedy. Some of our patients had not returned. In the confusion at the station one tramcar loaded with our patients had been sent off to another hospital by mistake. And the worst of it was that some of these were our favourite patients. There was nothing for it but to start next morning and make a tour of the hospitals in search of them. We were not long in finding them, for most of them were in a large hospital close by. I do not think we shall ever forget the reception we got when we found them. They had left us on stretchers, but they tried to get out of bed to come away with us, and one of them was a septic factured thigh with a hole in his leg into which you could put your fist, and another had recently had a serious abdominal operation. They seized our hands and would scarcely let us go until we had promised that as soon as we had arranged with the authorities they should come back to our hospital. It was managed after a little diplomacy, and they all came back next day, and we were again a united family.

XI

CONTICH

SUNDAY, the 4th of October, dawned with an extraordinary feeling of relief and expectancy in the air. The invincible British had arrived, huge guns were on their way, a vast body of French and British troops was advancing by forced marches, and would attack our besiegers in the rear, and beyond all possibility of doubt crush them utterly. But perhaps the most convincing proof of all was the round head of the First Lord of the Admiralty calmly having his lunch in the Hôtel St. Antoine. Surely nothing can inspire such confidence as the sight of an Englishman eating. It is one of the most substantial phenomena in nature, and certainly on this occasion I found the sight more convincing than a political speech. Obviously we were saved, and one felt a momentary pang of pity for the misguided Germans who had taken on such an impossible task. The sight of British troops in the streets and of three armoured cars carrying machine guns settled the question, and we went home to spread the good news and to follow the noble example of the First Lord.

In the afternoon three of us went off in one of the motors for a short run, partly to see if we could be of any use at the front with the wounded, and partly to see, if possible, the British troops. We took a stretcher with us, in case there should be any wounded to bring in from outlying posts. Everywhere we found signs of the confidence which the British had brought. It was visible in the face of every Belgian soldier, and even the children cheered our khaki uniforms as we passed. Everywhere there were signs of a new activity and of a new hope. The trenches and wire entanglements around the town, already very extensive, were being perfected, and to our eyes they looked impregnable. We did not then realize how useless it is to attempt to defend a town, and, unfortunately, our ignorance was not limited to civilians. It is a curious freak of modern war that a ploughed field should be stronger than any citadel. But, as I say, these things were hidden from us, and our allies gave the finishing touches to their trenches, to the high entertainment of the Angels, as Stevenson would have told us. If only those miles of trench and acres of barbed wire had been placed ten miles away, and backed by British guns, the story of Antwerp might have been a very different one.

The road to Boom is like all the main roads of Belgium. The central causeway was becoming worn by the constant passage of heavy motor lorries tearing backwards and forwards at racing speed. The sides were deep in dust, for there had been little rain. On each side rose poplars in ordered succession, and the long, straight stretches of the road were framed in the endless vista of their tall trunks. And in that frame moved a picture too utterly piteous for any words to describe—a whole country fleeing before the Huns. The huge unwieldy carts of the Belgian farmer crept slowly along, drawn by great Flemish horses. In front walked the men, plodding along beside the splendid animals, with whose help they had ploughed their fields—fields they would never see again. In the carts was piled up all that they possessed in the world, all that they could carry of their homes wrecked and blasted by the Vandals, a tawdry ornament or a child's toy looking out pitifully from the heap of clothes and bedding. And seated on the top of the heap were the woman and the children.

But these were the well-to-do. There were other little groups who had no cart and no horse. The father and a son would walk in front carrying all that a man could lift on their strong backs; then came the children, boys and girls, each with a little white bundle over their shoulder done up in a towel or a pillowslip, tiny mites of four or five doing all they could to save the home; and last came the mother with a baby at her breast, trudging wearily through the dust. They came in an endless stream, over and over again, for mile after mile, always in the same pathetic little groups, going away, only going away.

At last, with a sigh of relief, we reached Boom, and the end of the lines of refugees, for the Germans themselves were not far beyond. At the Croix Rouge we asked for instructions as to where we were likely to be useful. Boom had been shelled in the morning, but it was now quiet, and there was no fighting in the neighbourhood. We could hear the roar of guns in the distance on the east, and we were told that severe fighting was in progress in that direction. The British had reinforced the Belgian troops in the trenches at Duffel, and the Germans were attacking the position in force. Taking the road to the left, we passed the great brickfields which provide one of the chief industries of Boom, and we drove through the poorer portion of the town which lies amongst them. It was utterly deserted. It was in this part of the town that the shelling had been

HOMELESS.

Underwood phot.

most severe, but a large number of the shells must have fallen harmlessly in the brickfields, as only a house here and there was damaged. If, however, the object of the Germans was to clear the town of inhabitants, they had certainly succeeded, for there was not a man, woman, or child to be seen anywhere. It is a strange and uncanny thing to drive through a deserted town. Only a few days before we had driven the same way, and we had to go quite slowly to avoid the crowd in the streets. This time we crept along slowly, but for a very different reason. We distrusted those empty houses. We never knew what might be hiding round the next corner, but we did know that a false turning would take us straight into the German lines. It was the only way by which we could reach our destination, but we were beyond the main Belgian lines, and our road was only held by a few isolated outposts. After a mile or so we came upon a small outpost, and they told us that we should be safe as far as Rumps, about three miles farther, where their main outpost was placed. An occasional shell sailed over our heads to reassure us, some from our own batteries, and some from the enemy's. We only hoped that neither side would fire short.

At Rumps we found the headquarters of the regiment, and several hundred troops. At the sight of our khaki uniforms they at once raised a cheer, and we had quite an ovation as we passed down the street. At the Etat Majeur the Colonel himself came out to see us, and his officers crowded round as he asked us anxiously about the British arrivals. He pulled out his orders for the day, and told us the general disposition of the British and Belgian troops. He told us that the road to Duffel was too dangerous, and that we must turn northwards to Contich, but that there might be some wounded in the Croix Rouge station there. He and his men were typical of the Belgian Army —brave, simple men, defending their country as best they could, without fuss or show. I hope they have come to no harm. If only that army had been trained and equipped like ours, the Germans would have had a hard struggle to get through Belgium.

We turned away from the German lines northwards towards Contich. Our road lay across the open country, between the farms which mean so much of Belgium's wealth. In one field a man was ploughing with three big horses. He was too old to fight, but he could do this much for his country. Surely that man deserves a place in his country's Roll of Honour. Shells were falling not four fields away, but he never even looked up. It must take more nerve to plough a straight

CONTICH 99

furrow when the shells are falling than to aim a gun. I like to think of that man, and I hope that he will be left to reap his harvest in peace. A little farther on we came upon the objective of the German shells—a battery so skilfully concealed that it was only when we were close to it that we realized where it was. The ammunition-carts were drawn up in a long line behind a hedge, while the guns themselves were buried in piles of brushwood. They must have been invisible from the captive balloon which hung over the German lines in the distance. They were not firing when we passed, and we were not sorry, as we had no desire to be there when the replies came. An occasional shell gives a certain spice to the situation, but in quantity they are better avoided.

As we approached Contich a soldier came running up and told us that two people had just been injured by a shell, and begged us to come to see them. He stood on the step of the car, and directed us to a little row of cottages half a mile farther on. At the roadside was a large hole in the ground where a shell had fallen some minutes before, and beside it an unfortunate cow with its hind-quarters shattered. In the garden of the first cottage a poor woman lay on her back. She was dead, and her worn hands were already cold. As I rose from my knees a young soldier flung himself down beside her, sobbing as though his heart would break. She was his mother.

Behind the cottage we found a soldier with his left leg torn to fragments. He had lost a great deal of blood, and he was still bleeding from a large artery, in spite of the efforts of a number of soldiers round who were applying tourniquets without much success. The ordinary tourniquet is probably the most inefficient instrument that the mind of man could devise—at least, for dealing with wounds of the thigh out in the field. It might stop hæmorrhage in an infant, but for a burly soldier it is absurd. I tried two of the most approved patterns, and both broke in my hands. In the end I managed to stop it with a handkerchief and a stick. I would suggest the elimination of all tourniquets, and the substitution of the humble pocket-handkerchief. It, at least, does not pretend to be what it is not. Between shock and loss of blood our soldier was pretty bad, and we did not lose much time in transferring him to our car on a stretcher. The Croix Rouge dressing-station was more than a mile farther on, established in a large villa in its own grounds. We carried our man in, and laid him on a table with the object of dressing his leg properly, and of getting the man himself into such condition as would enable him to stand the journey back to

Antwerp. Alas! the dressing-station was destitute of any of the most elementary appliances for the treatment of a seriously wounded man. There was not even a fire, and the room was icy cold. There was no hot water, no brandy, no morphia, no splints, and only a minute quantity of dressing material. A cupboard with some prehistoric instruments in it was the only evidence of surgery that we could find. The Belgian doctor in charge was doing the best he could, but what he could be expected to do in such surroundings I do not know. He seemed greatly relieved to hear that I was a surgeon, and he was most kind in trying to find me everything for which I asked. From somewhere we managed to raise some brandy and hot water, and a couple of blankets, and with the dressings we had brought with us we made the best of a bad job, and started for home with our patient. Antwerp was eight miles away. It was a bitterly cold evening, and darkness was coming on. It seemed improbable that we could get our patient home alive, but it was perfectly certain that he would die if we left him where he was. It seemed such a pity that a little more forethought and common sense could not have been expended on that dressing-station, and yet we found that with rare exceptions this was the regular state of affairs, whether in Belgium or

France. It seems to be impossible for our professional brethren on the Continent to imagine any treatment apart from a completely equipped hospital. Their one idea seems to be to get the wounded back to a base hospital, and if they die on the way it cannot be helped. The dressing-stations are mere offices for their redirection, where they are carefully ticketed, but where little else is done. Of course, it is true that the combatant forces are the first consideration, and that from their point of view the wounded are simply in the way, and the sooner they are carried beyond the region of the fighting the better; but if this argument were carried to its logical conclusion, there should be no medical services at the front at all, except what might be absolutely necessary for the actual transport of the wounded. I am glad to say that our later experiences showed that the British influence was beginning to make itself felt, and that the idea of the wounded as a mere useless encumbrance was being modified by more humanitarian considerations. And in a long war it must be obvious to the most hardened militarist that by the early treatment of a wound many of its more severe consequences may be averted, and that many a man may thus be saved for further service. In a war of exhaustion, the ultimate result might well depend on how the wounded were treated in the field.

The road was crowded with traffic, and it was quite dark before we reached Antwerp. Our patient did not seem much the worse for his journey, though that is perhaps faint praise. We soon had him in our theatre, which was always warm and ready for cases such as this. With energetic treatment his condition rapidly improved, and when we left him to go to dinner we felt that our afternoon had not been entirely wasted.

XII

THE BOMBARDMENT—NIGHT

WE had had plenty of notice that we might expect a bombardment. On Saturday a boat had left with most of the English Colony. On Tuesday morning the Germans sent in official notice that they intended to bombard the city, and in the evening the Government and the Legations left by boat with the remainder of our countrymen who lived in Antwerp. We had faced the prospect and made every preparation for it, and yet when it did come it came upon us as a surprise. It is sometimes fortunate that our capacities for anticipation are so limited.

It was almost midnight on Wednesday, the 7th of October, and two of us were sitting in the office writing despatches home. The whole building was in absolute silence, and lit only by the subdued light of an occasional candle. In the distance we could hear the dull booming of the guns. Suddenly above our heads sounded a soft whistle, which was not the wind, followed by a dull thud in the distance. We looked at one another.

THE BOMBARDMENT—NIGHT

Again it came, this time a little louder. We ran up to the roof and stood there for some moments, fascinated by the scene. From the dull grey sky came just sufficient light to show the city laying in darkness around us, its tall spires outlined as dim shadows against the clouds. Not a sound arose from streets and houses around, but every few seconds there came from the south-east a distant boom, followed by the whistle of a shell overhead and the dull thud of its explosion. The whole scene was eerie and uncanny in the extreme. The whistle changed to a shriek and the dull thud to a crash close at hand, followed by the clatter of falling bricks cutting sharply into the stillness of the night. Plainly this was going to be a serious business, and we must take instant measures for the safety of our patients. At any moment a shell might enter one of the wards, and—well, we had seen the hospital at Lierre. We ran downstairs and told the night nurses to get the patients ready for removal, whilst we went across to the gymnasium to arouse those of the staff who slept there. We collected all our stretchers, and began the methodical removal of all our patients to the basement. In a few minutes there was a clang at the front-door bell, and our nurses and assistants who lived outside began to arrive. Two of the dressers had to come half a mile along the Malines road, where the shells were falling thickest, and every few yards they had had to shelter in doorways from the flying shrapnel. The bombardment had begun in earnest now, and shells were fairly pouring over our heads. We started with the top floor, helping down those patients who could walk, and carrying the rest on stretchers. When that was cleared we took the second, and I think we all breathed a sigh of relief when we heard that the top floor was empty. We were fortunate in having a basement large enough to accommodate all our patients, and wide staircases down which the stretchers could be carried without difficulty; but the patients were all full-grown men, and as most of them had to be carried it was hard work.

I shall never forget the scene on the great staircase, crowded with a long train of nurses, doctors, and dressers carrying the wounded down as gently and as carefully as if they were in a London hospital. I saw no sign of fear in any face, only smiles and laughter. And yet overhead was a large glass roof, and there was no one there who did not realize that a shell might come through that roof at any moment, and that it would not leave a single living person beneath it. It made one proud to have English blood running in one's veins. We had 113 wounded, and within an hour they were all in places of safety; mattresses

THE BOMBARDMENT—NIGHT

and blankets were brought, and they were all made as comfortable as possible for the night. Four were grave intestinal cases. Seven had terrible fractures of the thigh, but fortunately five of these had been already repaired with steel plates, and their transport was easy; in fact, I met one of them on the staircase, walking with the support of a dresser's arm, a week after the operation! Some of the patients must have suffered excruciating pain in being moved, but one never heard a murmur, and if a groan could not be kept back, it was passed over with a jest for fear we should notice it. It was a magnificent basement, with heavy arched roofs everywhere, and practically shell-proof. The long passages and the large kitchens were all tiled and painted white, and as the electric light was still running and the whole building was well warmed, it would have been difficult to find a more cheerful and comfortable place. Coffee was provided for everyone, and when I took a last look round the night nurses were taking charge as if nothing had happened, and the whole place was in the regular routine of an ordinary everyday hospital.

Upstairs there was an improvised meal in progress in the office, and after our two hours' hard work we were glad of it. It is really wonderful how cheerful a thing a meal is in the middle of the night, with plenty of hot coffee and a borrowed cake. It is one of the compensations of our life in hospital, and even shells are powerless to disturb it. After that, as we knew we should have a heavy day before us, we all settled down in the safest corners we could find to get what rest we could. The staircase leading up to the entrance hall was probably the safest spot in the building, covered as it was by a heavy arch, and it was soon packed with people in attitudes more or less restful. A ward with a comfortable bed seemed to me quite safe enough, and I spent the night with three equally hedonistic companions. At first we lay listening to the shells as they passed overhead, sometimes with the soft whistle of distance, and sometimes with the angry shriek of a shell passing near. Occasionally the shriek would drop to a low howl, the note of a steam siren as it stops, and then a deafening crash and the clatter of falling bricks and glass would warn us that we had only escaped by a few yards. But even listening to shells becomes monotonous, and my eyes gradually glued together, and I fell asleep.

When I awoke it was early morning, and daylight had just come. The shells were still arriving, but not so fast, and mostly at a much greater distance. But another sound came at intervals, and we had much discussion as to what it might

THE BOMBARDMENT—NIGHT

mean. Every three and a half minutes exactly there came two distant booms, but louder than usual, and then two terrific shrieks one after the other, exactly like the tearing of a giant sheet of calico, reminding us strongly of the famous scene in " Peter Pan." Away they went in the distance, and if we ever heard the explosion it was a long way off. They certainly sounded like shells fired over our heads from quite close, and at a very low elevation, and we soon evolved the comforting theory that they were from a pair of big British guns planted up the river, and firing over the town at the German trenches beyond. We even saw a British gunboat lying in the Scheldt, and unlimited reinforcements pouring up the river. Alas! it was only a couple of big German guns shelling the harbour and the arsenal; at least, that is the conclusion at which we have since arrived. But for some hours those shells were a source of great satisfaction and comfort. One can lie in bed with great contentment, I find, when it is the other people who are being shelled.

XIII
THE BOMBARDMENT—DAY

WE were up early in the morning, and our first business was to go round to the British Headquarters to find out what they intended to do, and what they expected of us as a British base hospital. If they intended to stay, and wished us to do likewise, we were quite prepared to do so, but we did not feel equal to the responsibility of keeping more than a hundred wounded in a position so obviously perilous. From shrapnel they were fairly safe in the basement, but from large shells or from incendiary bombs there is no protection. It is not much use being in a cellar if the house is burnt down over your head. So two of us started off in our motor to get news.

The Headquarters were in the Hôtel St. Antoine, at the corner of the Place Verte opposite to the Cathedral, so we had to go right across the town. We went by the Rue d'Argile and the Rue Leopold, and we had a fair opportunity of estimating the results of the night's bombardment. In the streets through which we passed it was really

THE BOMBARDMENT—DAY 111

astonishingly small. Cornices had been knocked off, and the fragments lay in the streets; a good many windows were broken, and in a few cases a shell had entered an attic and blown up the roof. Plainly only small shells had been used. We did not realize that many of the houses we passed were just beginning to get comfortably alight, and that there was no one to put out the fires that had only begun so far to smoulder. A few people were about, evidently on their way out of Antwerp, but the vast bulk of the population had already gone. It is said that the population of half a million numbered by the evening only a few hundreds. We passed a small fox terrier lying on the pavement dead, and somehow it has remained in my mind as a most pathetic sight. He had evidently been killed by a piece of shrapnel, and it seemed very unfair. But probably his people had left him, and he was better out of it.

We turned into the Marche aux Souliers, and drew up at the Hôtel St. Antoine, and as we stepped down from the car a shell passed close to us with a shriek, and exploded with a terrific crash in the house opposite across the narrow street. We dived into the door of the hotel to escape the falling débris. So far the shells had been whistling comfortably over our heads, but it was evident that the Germans were aiming at the British Headquarters, and that we had put our heads into the thick of it, for it was now positively raining shells all round us. But we scarcely noticed them in our consternation at what we found, for the British Staff had disappeared. We wandered through the deserted rooms which had been so crowded a few days before, but there was not a soul to be seen. They had gone, and left no address. At last an elderly man appeared, whom I took to be the proprietor, and all he could tell us was that there was no one but himself in the building. Of all the desolate spots in the world I think that an empty hotel is the most desolate, and when you have very fair reason to believe that a considerable number of guns are having a competition as to which can drop a shell into it first, it becomes positively depressing. We got into our car and drove down the Place de Meir to the Belgian Croix Rouge, where we hoped to get news of our countrymen, and there we were told that they had gone to the Belgian Etat Majeur near by. We had a few minutes' conversation with the President of the Croix Rouge, a very good friend of ours, tall and of striking appearance, with a heavy grey moustache. We asked him what the Croix Rouge would do. "Ah," he said, "we will stay to the last!" At that very moment a shell exploded with a deafening crash just outside in the Place de

THE BOMBARDMENT—DAY 113

Meir. I looked at the President, and he threw up his hands in despair and led the way out of the building. The Belgian Red Cross had finished its work.

At last at the Etat Majeur we found our Headquarters, and I sincerely hope that wherever General Paris, Colonel Bridges, and Colonel Seely go, they will always find people as pleased to see them as we were. They very kindly told us something of the situation, and said that, though they had every intention of holding Antwerp, they advised us to clear out, and they placed at our disposal four motor omnibuses for the transport of the wounded. So off we drove back to the hospital to make arrangements for evacuating. It was a lively drive, for I suppose that the Germans had had breakfast and had got to work again; at any rate, shells were coming in pretty freely, and we were happier when we could run along under the lee of the houses. However, we got back to the hospital safely enough, and there we held a council of war.

It was in the office, of course—the most risky room we could have chosen, I suppose—but somehow that did not seem to occur to anyone. It is curious how soon one grows accustomed to shells. At that moment a barrel-organ would have caused us far more annoyance. We sat round the table and discussed the situation. It was by no means straightforward. In the first place several members of the community did not wish to leave at all; in the second, we could not leave any of our wounded behind unattended; and in the third, it seemed unlikely that we could get them all on to four buses. After a long discussion we decided to go again and see General Paris, to ask for absolute instructions as a hospital under his control, and if he told us to go, to get sufficient transport. And then arose a scene which will always live in my mind. We had impressed into consultation a retired officer of distinction to whose help we owed much, and now owe far more, and whom I shall call our Friend. Perhaps he wished to give us confidence—I have always suspected that he had an ulterior motive—but he concluded the discussion by saying that he felt hungry and would have something to eat before he started, and from his haversack he produced an enormous German sausage and a large loaf of bread, which he offered to us all round, and he said he would like a cup of tea! The shells could do what they liked outside, and if one of them was rude enough to intrude, it could not be helped. We must show them that we could pay no attention to anything so vulgar and noisy. At any rate, the effect on us was electrical. The contrast between the German shells

THE BOMBARDMENT—DAY 115

and the German sausage was too much for us, and the meeting broke up in positive confusion. Alas! that sausage, the unparalleled trophy of an incomparable moment, was left behind on the table, and I fear the Germans got it.

General Paris had been obliged to shift his headquarters to the Pilotage, on the docks and at the farthest end of the city from us. He was very considerate, and after some discussion said that we had better leave Antwerp, and sent Colonel Farquharson with us to get six buses. The Pilotage is at the extreme north end of the Avenue des Arts, which extends the whole length of Antwerp, and the buses were on the quay by the Arsenal at the extreme south end, so that we had to drive the whole length of this, the most magnificent street of Antwerp, and a distance of about three miles. It was an extraordinary drive. In the whole length of that Avenue I do not think that we passed a single individual. It was utterly deserted. All around were signs of the bombardment—tops of houses blown off, and scattered about the street, trees knocked down, holes in the roadway where shells had struck. On the left stood the great Palais de Justice, with most of its windows broken and part of the roof blown away, and just beyond this three houses in a row blazing from cellar to chimney, the front wall gone, and all that remained of the rooms exposed. As I said, only small shells had been used, and the damage was nothing at all to that which we afterwards saw at Ypres; but it gave one an impression of dreariness and utter desolation that could scarcely be surpassed. Think of driving from Hyde Park Corner down the Strand to the Bank, not meeting a soul on the way, passing a few clubs in Piccadilly burning comfortably, the Cecil a blazing furnace, and the Law Courts lying in little bits about the street, and you will get some idea of what it looked like. The scream of the shells and the crash when they fell near by formed quite a suitable if somewhat Futurist accompaniment.

But the climax of the entertainment, the *bonne bouche* of the afternoon, was reserved for the end of our drive, when we reached the wharf by the Arsenal, where the British stores and transport were collected. Here was a long row of motor-buses, about sixty of them, all drawn up in line along the river. Beside them was a long row of heavily loaded ammunition lorries, and on the other side of the road was the Arsenal, on our left, blazing away, with a vast column of smoke towering up to the sky. "It may blow up any minute," said Colonel Farquharson cheerily, "I had better move that ammunition." I have never seen an

ANTWERP—AFTER THE BOMBARDMENT.

Underwood phot.

THE BOMBARDMENT—DAY 117

arsenal blow up, and I imagine it is a phenomenon requiring distance to get it into proper perspective; but I have some recollection of an arsenal blowing up in Antwerp a few years ago and taking a considerable part of the town with it. However, it was not *our* arsenal, so we waited and enjoyed the view till the ammunition had been moved, and the Colonel had done his best to get us the motor-buses. He could only get us four, so we had to make the best of a bad job. But meanwhile the Germans had evidently determined to give us a really good show while they were about it, for while we waited a Taube came overhead and hovered for a moment, apparently uncertain as to whether a bomb or a shell would look better just there. A flash of tinsel falling in the sunlight showed us that she had made up her mind and was giving the range. But we could not stay, and were a quarter of a mile away when we looked back and saw the first shells falling close to where we had been two minutes before. They had come six miles.

The bombardment was increasing in violence, and large numbers of incendiary shells were being used, whilst in addition the houses set on fire during the night were now beginning to blaze. As we drove back we passed several houses in flames, and the passage of the narrow streets we traversed was by no means free from risk. At last we turned into our own street, the Boulevard Leopold, and there we met a sight which our eyes could scarcely credit. Three motor-buses stood before our door and patients were being crowded into them. Those buses and our own lives we owe to the kindness of Major Gordon. Without them some at least must have remained behind. The three were already well filled, for our friends thought that we had certainly been killed and that they must act for themselves. We sent them off under the escort of one of our cars, as it seemed foolish to keep them waiting in a position of danger. On our own four we packed all our remaining patients and all the hospital equipment we could remove. One does not waste time when one packs under shell fire, and at the end of three-quarters of an hour there was not a patient and very little of value in the hospital. I took charge of the theatre as I knew where the things went, and I think the British working man would have been rather astonished to see how fast the big sterilizers fell apart and the operating-tables slid into their cases. The windows faced shellwards, and I must confess that once or twice when one of them seemed to be coming unpleasantly near I took the opportunity to remove my parcels outside. How the patients were got ready and

THE BOMBARDMENT—DAY

carried out and into the buses in that time is beyond my comprehension. But somehow it was managed. I took a last look round and drove out the last nurse who was trying to rescue some last " hospital comfort " for a patient, and in the end I was myself driven out by two indignant dressers who caught me trying to save the instrument sterilizer. The buses were a wonderful sight. Inside were some sixty patients, our share of the whole hundred and thirteen, and on top about thirty of our staff, and the strangest collection of equipment imaginable. The largest steam sterilizer mounted guard in front, hoisted there by two sailormen of huge strength, who turned up from somewhere. Great bundles of blankets, crockery, and instruments were wedged in everywhere, with the luggage of the staff. At the door of each bus was seated a nurse, like a conductor, to give what little attention was possible to the patients. It was a marvellous sight, but no cheerier crowd of medical students ever left the doors of a hospital for a Cup-tie.

XIV

THE NIGHT JOURNEY

There was only one way out—by the bridge of boats across the Scheldt. It was a narrow plank road, and as vehicles had to go across in single file at some distance apart, the pressure can be imagined. For an hour and a half we stood in the densely packed Cathedral square watching the hands of the great clock go round and wondering when a shell would drop among us. We had seen enough of churches to know what an irresistible attraction they have for German artillery, and we knew that, whatever may be the state of affairs in Scotland, here at any rate the nearer the church the nearer was heaven. But no shells fell near, we only heard them whistling overhead.

The scene around us was extraordinary, and indeed these were the remains of the entire population of Antwerp. The whole city had emptied itself either by this road or by the road northwards into Holland. Crowds of people of every class—the poor in their working-clothes, the well-to-do in their Sunday best—all carrying in bundles all they could carry away of their property, and wedged in amongst them every kind of vehicle imaginable, from a luxurious limousine to coster's carts and wheelbarrows. In front of us lay the Scheldt, and pouring down towards it was on the left an endless stream of fugitives, crossing by the ferry-boats, and on the right an interminable train of artillery and troops, crossing by the only bridge. At last there was a movement forwards; we crept down the slope and on to the bridge, and slowly moved over to the other side. Perhaps we should not have felt quite so happy about it had we known that two men had just been caught on the point of blowing up the boats in the centre, and that very shortly after the Germans were to get the range and drop a shell on to the bridge. At five o'clock we were across the bridge and on the road to Ghent.

Of all the pitiful sights I have ever seen, that road was the most utterly pitiful. We moved on slowly through a dense throng of fugitives—men, women, and little children—all with bundles over their shoulders, in which was all that they possessed. A woman with three babies clinging to her skirts, a small boy wheeling his grandmother in a wheelbarrow, family after family, all moving away from the horror that lay behind to the misery that lay in front. We had heard of Louvain, and we had seen Termonde, and we understood. As darkness came down we lit our lamps, and there along the roadside sat rows of fugitives, resting before recommencing their long journey through the night. There was one row of little children which will live for ever in my memory, tiny mites sitting together on a bank by the roadside. We only saw them for an instant as our lights fell on them, and they disappeared in the darkness. Germany will have to pay for Louvain and Termonde. It is not with man that she will have to settle for that row of little children.

We had a few vacant seats when we left Antwerp, but they were soon filled by fugitives whom we picked up on the road. Strangely enough, we picked up two of our friends in Antwerp with their families. One was the doctor who had taken all our radiographs for us, and to whom we owed a great deal in many ways. He had left his beautiful house, with X-ray apparatus on which he had spent his fortune, incomparably superior to any other that I have ever seen, and here he was trudging along the road, with his wife, his two children, and their nurse. They were going to St. Nicholas, on their way to Holland, and were delighted to get a lift. Unfortunately, by some mistake, the nurse and children left the bus at Zwyndrecht, a few miles from Antwerp, the doctor came on to St. Nicholas, and his wife went right through with us to Ghent. It took him three days to find the children, and when we last heard from him he was in Holland, having lost everything he had in the world, and after two months he had not yet found his wife. And this is only an instance of what has happened all over Belgium.

We reached St. Nicholas about eight o'clock, having covered thirteen miles in three hours. It was quite dark, and as we had a long night before us we decided to stop and get some food for ourselves and our patients. There was not much to be had, but, considering the stream of fugitives, it was wonderful that there was anything. We hoped now to be able to push on faster, and to reach Ghent before midnight, for it is only a little over twenty miles by the direct road. To our dismay, we found that Lokeren, half-way to Ghent, was in the hands of the Germans, and that we must make a détour, taking us close to the Dutch border, and nearly doubling the distance. Without a guide, and in the dark, we could never have reached our destination; but we were fortunate enough to get a guide, and we set out on our long drive through the night. Twenty minutes later a German scouting party entered St. Nicholas. It was a narrow margin, but it was sufficient.

We were rather a downhearted party when we set out northwards towards the Dutch frontier, for we had been told that the three buses we had sent on in advance had gone straight on to Lokeren, and had undoubtedly fallen into the hands of the Germans, who had made certain of holding the road by destroying the bridge. We hoped that they might have discovered this in time, and turned back, but we could not wait to find out. We knew that the enemy were quite close. At first we used our lights, but a shrapnel whistling overhead warned us that we were seen, and for the remainder of the night we travelled in darkness. These were minor roads, with a narrow paved causeway in the centre, and loose sand on each side. Long avenues of trees kept us in inky darkness, and how the drivers succeeded in keeping on the causeway I really do not know. Every now and then one of the buses would get into the sand; then all the men would collect, dig the wheels clear, and by sheer brute force drag the bus back to safety. Twice it seemed absolutely hopeless. The wheels were in the loose sand within a foot of a deep ditch, and the least thing would have sent the bus flying over on to its side into the field beyond; and on both occasions, while we looked at one another in despair, a team of huge Flemish horses appeared from nowhere in the darkness and dragged us clear. Think of an inky night, the Germans close at hand, and every half-hour or so a desperate struggle to shoulder a heavily loaded London bus out of a ditch, and you may have some faint idea of the nightmare we passed through.

As we crept along the dark avenues, the sky behind us was lit by an ever-increasing glare. Away to the south-east, at no great distance, a village was blazing, but behind us was a vast column of flame and smoke towering up to heaven. It was in the direction of Antwerp, and at first we thought that the vandals had fired the town; but though the sky was lit by many blazing houses, that tall pillar came from the great oil-tanks, set on fire by the Belgians lest they should fall into German hands. A more awful and terrifying spectacle it is hard to conceive. The sky was lit up as if by the sunrise of the day of doom, and thirty miles away our road was lighted by the lurid glare. Our way led through woods, and amongst the trees we could hear the crack and see the flash of rifle-fire. More than once the whiz of a bullet urged us to hurry on.

At Selsaete, only a mile from the Dutch frontier, we turned southwards towards Ghent, and for an interminable distance we followed the bank of a large canal. A few miles from Ghent we met

Commander Samson, of the Flying Corps, and three of his armoured cars. The blaze of their headlights quite blinded us after the darkness in which we had travelled, but the sight of the British uniforms and the machine guns was a great encouragement. The road was so narrow that they had to turn their cars into a field to let us pass. We had just come up with a number of farm waggons, and the clumsy Flemish carts, with their huge horses, the grey armoured cars, with their blazing headlights, and our four red motor-buses, made a strange scene in the darkness of the night. At last we reached Ghent utterly tired out, though personally I had slept a sort of nightmare sleep on the top step of a bus which boldly announced its destination as Hendon. It was five o'clock, and day was breaking as we got our patients out of the buses and deposited them in the various hospitals as we could find room for them. To our unspeakable relief, we found that the rest of our party had come through by much the same road as we had taken ourselves, but they had reached Ghent quite early the night before. Their earlier start had given them the advantage of clearer roads and daylight. With good fortune little short of miraculous, we had all come so far in safety, and we hoped that our troubles were over. Alas! we were told that the

Germans were expected to enter Ghent that very day, and that all British wounded must be removed from the hospitals before ten o'clock. There was nothing for it but to collect them again, and to take them on to Ostend. One had died in the night, and two were too ill to be moved. We left them behind in skilled hands, and the others we re-embarked on our buses *en route* for Bruges and Ostend.

The First Act in the story of the British Field Hospital for Belgium was drawing to an end. Our hospital, to which we had given so much labour, was gone, and the patients, for whom we had grown to care, were scattered. Yet there was in our hearts only a deep gratitude that we had come unharmed, almost by a miracle, through so many dangers, and a firm confidence that in some other place we should find a home for our hospital, where we could again help the brave soldiers whose cause had become so much our own.

XV

FURNES

A WEEK after we had reached London, we were off again to the front. This time our objective was Furnes, a little town fifteen miles east of Dunkirk, and about five miles from the fighting-line. The line of the Belgian trenches ran in a circle, following the course of the River Yser, the little stream which has proved such an insuperable barrier to the German advance. Furnes lies at the centre of the circle, and is thus an ideal position for an advanced base, such as we intended to establish. It is easy of access from Dunkirk by a fine main road which runs alongside an important canal, and as Dunkirk was our port, and the only source of our supplies, this was a great consideration. From Furnes a number of roads lead in various directions to Ypres, Dixmude, Nieuport, and the coast, making it a convenient centre for an organization such as ours, requiring, as we did, ready means of reaching the front in any direction, and open communication with our base of supplies.

The Surgical Staff. Furnes.

FURNES 129

We crossed from Dover in the Government transport, and arrived at Dunkirk about ten o'clock on Tuesday morning. There we met Dr. Munro's party, the famous Flying Ambulance Corps, with whom we were to enter on our new venture. They had not come over to England at all, but had come down the coast in their cars, and had spent the last few days in Malo, the seaside suburb of Dunkirk. The Belgian Government very kindly lent us a couple of big motor-lorries in which to take out our stores, and with our own motors we made quite a procession as we started off from the wharf of Dunkirk on our fifteen-mile drive to Furnes. It was late in the afternoon when we reached our new home. It was a large school, partly occupied by the priests connected with it, partly by officers quartered there, and one of the larger classrooms had been used as a dressing-station by some Belgian doctors in Furnes. For ourselves, the only accommodation consisted of a few empty classrooms and a huge dormitory divided into cubicles, but otherwise destitute of the necessaries for sleep. Several hours' hard work made some change in the scene, mattresses and blankets being hauled up to the dormitory, where the nursing staff was accommodated, while straw laid down in one of the classrooms made comfortable if somewhat primitive beds for the male members. Meanwhile, in the kitchen department miracles had been accomplished, and we all sat down to dinner with an appetite such as one rarely feels at home, and for which many of our patients over in England would be willing to pay quite large sums. The large room was lit by two candles and a melancholy lamp, there was no tablecloth, the spoons were of pewter, with the bowls half gone, and the knives were in their dotage. But the scales had fallen from our eyes, and we realized what trifles these things are. Madame, the genius who presided over our domestic affairs, and many other affairs as well, and her assistants, had produced from somewhere food, good food, and plenty of it; and what in the world can a hungry man want more? Truly there are many people who require a moral operation for cataract, that they might see how good is the world in which they live.

Next day we proceeded to unpack our stores, and to try to make a hospital out of these empty rooms, and then only did we discover that an overwhelming misfortune had overtaken us. By some extraordinary circumstance which has never been explained, we had lost practically the whole of the surgical instruments which we had brought out of Antwerp with such trouble and risk. They were tied up in sheets, and my own impression is that they were stolen. However that may be, here we were in as ludicrous a position as it is possible for even a hospital to occupy, for not only had we none of the ordinary instruments, but, as if Fate meant to have a good laugh at us, we had a whole series of rare and expensive tools. We had no knives, and no artery forceps, and not a stitch of catgut; but we had an œsophagoscope, and the very latest possible pattern of cystoscope, and a marvellous set of tools for plating fractures. It reminded one of the costume of an African savage—a silk hat, and nothing else. Some Belgian doctors who had been working there lent us a little case of elementary instruments, and that was absolutely all we had.

Scarcely had we made this terrible discovery, when an ambulance arrived with two wounded officers, and asked if we were ready to admit patients. We said, "No," and I almost think that we were justified. The men in charge of the ambulance seemed very disappointed, and said that in that case there was nothing for it but to leave the wounded men on their stretchers till an ambulance train should come to take them to Calais, which they might ultimately reach in two or three days' time. They were badly wounded, and we thought that at least we could do better than that; so we made up a couple of beds in one of the empty rooms, and took them in. Little did we dream of what we were in for. An hour later another ambulance arrived, and as we had started, we thought that we might as well fill up the ward we had begun. That did it. The sluice-gates were opened, and the wounded poured in. In four days we admitted three hundred and fifty patients, all of them with injuries of the most terrible nature. The cases we had seen at Antwerp were nothing to these. Arms and legs were torn right off or hanging by the merest shreds, ghastly wounds of the head left the brain exposed. Many of the poor fellows were taken from the ambulances dead, and of the others at least half must have died. For four days and four nights the operating theatre was at work continuously, till one sickened at the sight of blood and at the thought of an operation. Three operating tables were in almost continuous use, and often three major operations were going on at the same time; and all the instruments we had were two scalpels, six artery forceps, two dissecting forceps, and a finger-saw. Think of doing amputations through the thigh with that equipment! There was nothing else for it. Either the work had to be done or the patients had to die. And there was certainly no one else to do it.

The rapid advance of the Germans had swept

DINNER. FURNES.

THE COURTYARD. FURNES.

away all the admirable arrangements which the Belgian Army had made for dealing with its wounded. The splendid hospitals of Ghent and Ostend were now in German hands, and there had not yet been time to get new ones established. The cases could be sent to Calais, it was true, but there the accommodation was so far totally inadequate, and skilled surgical assistance was not to be obtained. For the moment our hospital, with its ludicrous equipment, was the only hope of the badly wounded. By the mercy of Heaven, we had plenty of chloroform and morphia, and a fair supply of dressings, and we knew by experience that at this stage it is safer to be content with the minimum of actual operative work, so that I think it was we, rather than our patients, who suffered from the want of the ordinary aids of surgery. In the wards there was a shortage, almost as serious, of all the ordinary equipment of nursing, for much of this had been too cumbrous to bring from Antwerp; and though we had brought out a fair supply of ordinary requirements, we had never dreamt of having to deal with such a rush as this. Ward equipment cannot be got at a moment's notice, and the bulk of it had not yet arrived. We only possessed a dozen folding beds, in which some of the worst cases were placed. The others had to lie on straw on the floor, and so closely were they packed that it was only with the greatest care that one could thread one's way across the ward. How the nurses ever managed to look after their patients is beyond my comprehension, but they were magnificent. They rose to the emergency as only Englishwomen can, and there is not one of those unfortunate men who will not remember with gratitude their sympathy and their skill.

During these first days a terrific fight was going on around Dixmude and Nieuport, and it was a very doubtful question how long it would be possible for the Belgian and French troops to withstand the tremendous attacks to which they were being subjected. The matter was so doubtful that we had to hold ourselves in readiness to clear out from the hospital at two hours' notice, whilst our wounded were taken away as fast as we could get them into what one can only describe as a portable condition. It was a physical impossibility for our wards to hold more than a hundred and fifty patients, even when packed close together side by side on the floor, and as I have said, three hundred and fifty were dealt with in the first four days. This meant that most of them spent only twenty-four hours in the hospital, and as we were only sent cases which could not, as they stood, survive the long train journey to Calais, this

FURNES 135

meant that they were often taken on almost immediately after serious operations. Several amputations of the thigh, for example, were taken away next day, and many of them must have spent the next twenty-four hours in the train, for the trains were very tardy in reaching their destination. It is not good treatment, but good surgery is not the primary object of war. The fighting troops are the first consideration, and the surgeon has to manage the best way he can.

One of the most extraordinary cases we took in was that of the editor of a well-known sporting journal in England. He had shown his appreciation of the true sporting instinct by going out to Belgium and joining the army as a mitrailleuse man. If there is one place where one may hope for excitement, it is in an armoured car with a mitrailleuse. The mitrailleuse men are picked dare-devils, and their work takes them constantly into situations which require a trained taste for their enjoyment. Our friend the editor was out with his car, and had got out to reconnoitre, when suddenly some Germans in hiding opened fire. Their first shot went through both his legs, fracturing both tibiæ, and he fell down, of course absolutely incapable of standing, just behind the armoured car. Owing to some mistake, an officer in the car gave the order to start, and away went the car. He would have been left to his fate, but suddenly realizing how desperate his position was, he threw up his hand and caught hold of one of the rear springs. Lying on his back and holding on to the spring, he was dragged along the ground, with both his legs broken, for a distance of about half a mile. The car was going at about twenty-five miles an hour, and how he ever maintained his hold Heaven only knows. At last they pulled up, and there they found him, practically unconscious, his clothes torn to ribbons, his back a mass of bruises, but still holding on. It was one of the most splendid examples of real British grit of which I have ever heard. They brought him to the hospital, and we fixed him up as well as we could. One would have thought that he might have been a little downhearted, but not a bit of it. He arrived in the operating theatre smiling and smoking a cigar, and gave us a vivid account of his experiences. We sent him over to England, and I heard that he was doing well. There is one sporting paper in England which is edited by a real sportsman. May he long live to inspire in others the courage of which he has given such a splendid example!

XVI

POPERINGHE

FOR a long week the roar of guns had echoed incessantly in our corridors and wards, and a continuous stream of motor-lorries, guns, and ammunition waggons had rumbled past our doors; whilst at night the flash of the guns lit up the horizon with an angry glare. The flood of wounded had abated, and we were just beginning to get the hospital into some sort of shape when the order came to evacuate.

It had been no easy task transforming bare rooms into comfortable wards, arranging for supplies of food and stores, and fitting a large staff into a cubic space totally inadequate to hold them. But wonderful things can be accomplished when everyone is anxious to do their share, and the most hopeless sybarite will welcome shelter however humble, and roll himself up in a blanket in any corner, when he is dead tired. For the first few days the rush of wounded had been so tremendous that all we could do was to try to keep our heads above water and not be drowned by the flood.

But towards the end of the week the numbers diminished, not because there were not as many wounded, but because the situation was so critical that the Belgian authorities did not dare to leave any large number of wounded in Furnes. Supplies were coming out from England in response to urgent telegrams, and, through the kind offices of the Queen of the Belgians, we had been able to obtain a number of beds from the town, in addition to twenty which she had generously given to us herself. So that we were gradually beginning to take on the appearance of an ordinary hospital, and work was settling down into a regular routine.

The sleepy little town of Furnes had been for some weeks in a state of feverish activity. After the evacuation of Antwerp and the retirement of the Belgian Army from Ostend, it had become the advanced base of the Belgian troops, and it was very gay with Staff officers, and of course packed with soldiers. The immense Grand Place lined with buildings, in many cases bearing unmistakable signs of a birth in Spanish times, was a permanent garage of gigantic dimensions, and the streets were thronged day and night with hurrying cars. We in the hospital hoped that the passage of the Yser would prove too much for the Germans, and that we should be left in peace, for we could not bear to think that all our labour could be thrown to the winds, and that we might have to start afresh in some other place. But one of the massed attacks which have formed such a prominent feature of this terrible war had temporarily rolled back the defence in the Dixmude district, and it was deemed unwise to submit the hospital to the risk of possible disaster.

We were fortunate in having Dr. Munro's ambulance at our disposal, and in rather over two hours more than a hundred wounded had been transferred to the Red Cross train which lay at the station waiting to take them to Calais. An evacuation is always a sad business, for the relations between a hospital and its patients are far more than professional. But with us it was tragic, for we knew that for many of our patients the long journey could have only one conclusion. Only the worst cases were ever brought to us, in fact only those whose condition rendered the long journey to Calais a dangerous proceeding, and we felt that for many of them the evacuation order was a death warrant, and that we should never see them again. They were brave fellows, and made the best of it as they shook hands with smiling faces and wished us " Au revoir," for though they might die on the way they preferred that to the danger of falling into the hands of the Germans. And they were right. They knew as well as we did that we are not fighting against a civilized nation, but against a gang of organized savages.

Three hours later we were mingling with the crowds who thronged the road, wondering with them where our heads would rest that night, and filled with pity at the terrible tragedy which surrounded us. Carts, wheelbarrows, perambulators, and in fact any vehicle which could be rolled along, were piled to overflowing with household goods. Little children and old men and women struggled along under loads almost beyond their powers, none of them knowing whither they went or what the curtain of fate would reveal when next it was drawn aside. It was a blind flight into the darkness of the unknown.

Our orders were to make for Poperinghe, a little town lying about fifteen miles due south of Furnes, in the direction of Ypres. For the first ten miles we travelled along the main road to Ypres, a fine avenue running between glorious trees, and one of the chief thoroughfares of Belgium. Here we made our first acquaintance with the African troops, who added a touch of colour in their bright robes to the otherwise grey surroundings. They were encamped in the fields by the side of the road, and seemed to be lazily enjoying themselves seated round their camp-fires. At Oostvleteren we parted company with the main road and its fine surface, and for the next six miles we bumped and jolted along on a bad cross-road till our very bones rattled and groaned.

There was no suggestion now of the horrors of war. Peaceful villages as sleepy as any in our own country districts appeared at frequent intervals, and easy prosperity was the obvious keynote of the well-wooded and undulating countryside. We were in one of the great hop districts, and the contrast with the flat and unprotected country round Furnes was striking. One might almost have been in the sheltered hopfields of Kent. Little children looked up from their games in astonishment as we rolled by, and our response to their greetings was mingled with a silent prayer that they might be spared the terrible fate which had befallen their brothers and sisters in far-off Louvain. The contrasts of war are amazing. Here were the children playing by the roadside, and the cattle slowly wending their way home, and ten miles away we could hear the roar of the guns, and knew that on those wasted fields men were struggling with savage fury in one of the bloodiest battles of the war.

In the great square of Poperinghe the scene was brilliant in the extreme. Uniforms of every conceivable cut and colour rubbed shoulder to shoulder; ambulance waggons, guns, ammunition trains, and picketed horses all seemed to be mixed in inextricable confusion; while a squadron of French cavalry in their bright blue and silver uniforms was drawn up on one side of the square, waiting patiently for the orders which would permit them to go to the help of their hard-pressed comrades. It seemed impossible that we could find shelter here, for obviously every corner must have been filled by the throng of soldiers who crowded in the square. But we were quite happy, for had we not got Madame with us, and had her genius ever been known to fail, especially in the face of the impossible? Others might go without a roof, but not we, and others might go to bed supperless, but in some miraculous way we knew that we should sit down to a hot dinner. We were not deceived. The whole nursing staff was soon comfortably housed in a girls' school, while the men were allotted the outhouse of a convent, and there, rolled up in our blankets and with our bags for pillows, we slept that night as soundly as we should have done in our own comfortable beds in England.

There was ample room in the courtyard for our heavily laden ambulances, for we had brought all our stores with us; and a big pump was a welcome sight, for grime had accumulated during the preceding twelve hours. By the side of the friendly pump, in a railed-off recess, a life-size image of Our Lady of Lourdes, resplendent in blue and gold, looked down with a pitying smile on a group of pilgrims, one of whom bore a little child in her arms; whilst a well-worn stone step spoke of the number of suppliants who had sought her aid.

We had fasted for many hours, and while we were doing our part in unpacking the small store of food which we had brought with us, Madame, with her usual genius, had discovered on the outskirts of Poperinghe an obscure café, where for a small sum the proprietor allowed us to use his kitchen. There we were presently all seated round three tables, drinking coffee such as we had rarely tasted, and eating a curiously nondescript, but altogether delightful, meal. There were two little rooms, one containing a bar and a stove, the other only a table. Over the stove presided a lady whose novels we have all read, cooking bacon, and when I say that she writes novels as well as she cooks bacon it is very high praise indeed—at least we thought so at the time. Some genius had discovered a naval store in the town, and had persuaded the officer in charge to give us cheese and jam and a whole side of bacon, so that we fed like the gods. There was one cloud over the scene, for the terrible discovery was made that we had left behind in Furnes a large box of sausages, over the fate of which it is well to draw a veil; but Madame was not to be defeated even by that, and a wonderful salad made of biscuits and vinegar and oil went far to console us. And that reminds me of a curious episode in Furnes. For several days the huge store bottle of castor oil was lost. It was ultimately discovered in the kitchen, where, as the label was in English, it had done duty for days as salad oil! What is there in a name after all?

We had not been able to bring with us all our stores, and as some of these were wanted two of us started back to Furnes late at night to fetch them. It was a glorious night, and one had the advantage of a clear road. We were driving northwards, and the sky was lit up by the flashes of the guns at Nieuport and Dixmude, whilst we could hear their dull roar in the distance. All along the road were encamped the Turcos, and their camp-fires, with the dark forms huddled around them, gave a picturesque touch to the scene. Half-way to Furnes the road was lit up by a motor-car which had caught fire, and which stood blazing in the middle of the road. We had some little difficulty in passing it, but when we

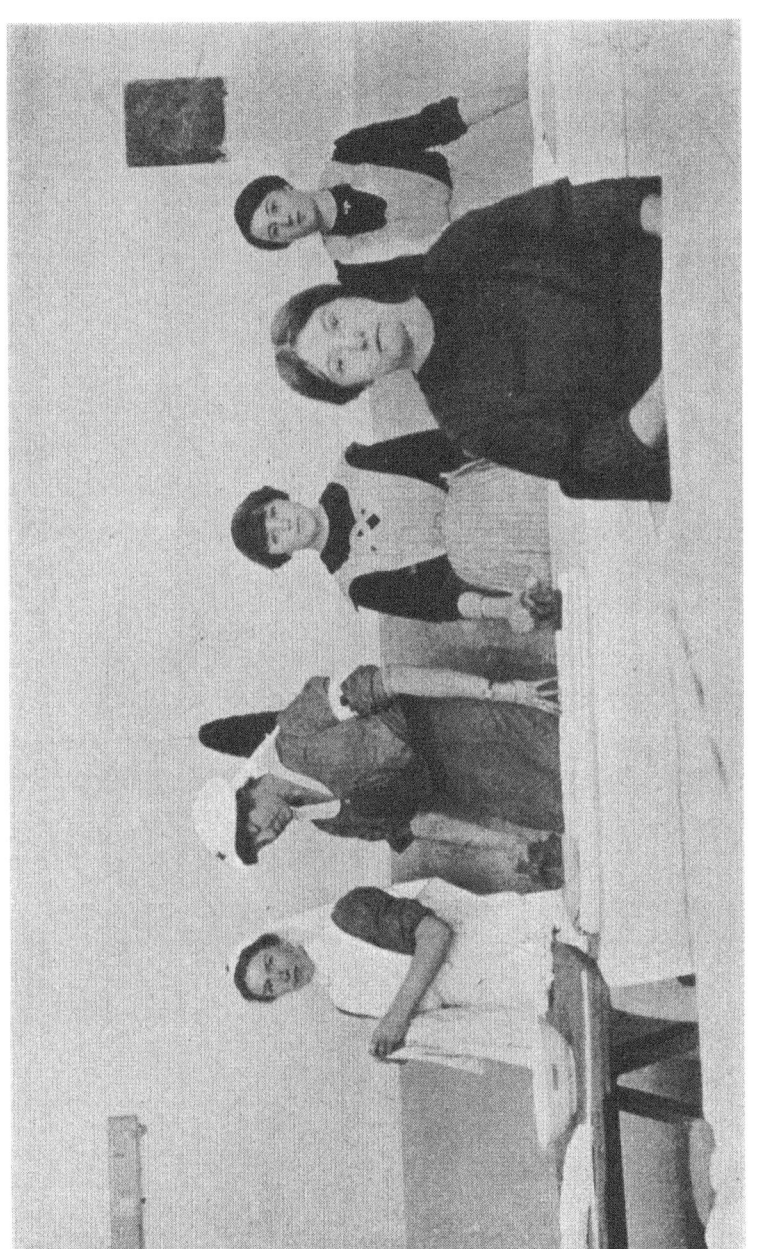

The Laundry. Furnes.

returned it was only a mass of twisted iron by the roadside. There was no moon, but the stars shone out all the more brilliantly as we spun along on the great Ypres road. It was long after midnight when we reached the hospital, and it was not a little uncanny groping through its wards in the darkness. There is some influence which seems to haunt the empty places where men once lived, but it broods in redoubled force over the places where men have died. In those wards, now so dark and silent, we had worked for all the past days amid sights which human eyes should never have seen, and the groans of suffering we had heard seemed to echo through the darkness. We were glad when we had collected the stores we required and were again in the car on our way back to Poperinghe.

Next morning we called at the Hôtel de Ville in Poperinghe, and there we learnt that the Queen, with her usual thoughtfulness, was interesting herself on our behalf to find us a building in which we could make a fresh start. She had sent the Viscomtesse de S. to tell us that she hoped to shortly place at our disposal either a school or a convent. On the following day, however, we heard that the situation had somewhat settled, and an order came from General Mellis, the Chief of the Medical Staff, instructing us to return to

Furnes. A few hours later found us hard at work again, putting in order our old home.

There was one rather pathetic incident of our expedition to Poperinghe. Five nuns who had fled from Eastern Belgium—they had come, I think, from a convent near Louvain—had taken refuge in the school in Furnes in which we were established. When we were ordered to go to Poperinghe, they begged to be allowed to accompany us, and we took them with us in the ambulances. On our return they were so grateful that they asked to be allowed to show their gratitude by working for us in the kitchen, and for all the time we were at Furnes they were our devoted helpers. They only made one request, that if we left Furnes we would take them with us, and we promised that we would never desert them.

XVII

FURNES AGAIN

THE position of the hospital at Furnes was very different from that which it had held at Antwerp. There we were in a modern city, with a water-supply and modern sanitary arrangements. Here we were in an old Continental country town, or, in other words, in medieval times, as far as water and sanitation were concerned. For it is only where the English tourist has penetrated that one can possibly expect such luxuries. One does not usually regard him as an apostle of civilization, but he ought certainly to be canonized as the patron saint of continental sanitary engineering. As a matter of fact, in a country as flat as Belgium the science must be fraught with extraordinary difficulties, and they certainly seem to thrive very well without it. We were established in the Episcopal College of St. Joseph, a large boys' school, and not badly adapted to the needs of a hospital but for the exceptions I have mentioned. Our water-supply came, on a truly hygienic plan, from wells beneath the building, whilst we were entirely free from any worry about drains. There were none. However, it did not seem to affect either ourselves or our patients, and we all had the best of health, though we took the precaution of sterilizing our water.

We were now the official advanced base hospital of the Belgian Army, and not merely, as in Antwerp, a free organization working by itself. The advantage of this arrangement was that we had a constant supply of wounded sent to us whenever there was any fighting going on, and that the evacuation of our patients was greatly facilitated. Every morning at ten o'clock Colonel Maestrio made the tour of our wards, and arranged for the removal to the base hospital at Dunkirk of all whom we wished to send away. It gave us the further advantage of special privileges for our cars and ambulances, which were allowed to go practically anywhere in search of the wounded with absolute freedom. Formerly we had owed a great deal to the assistance of the Belgian Croix Rouge, who had been very good in supplementing our supply of dressings, as well as in getting us army rations for the patients. This, of course, had all come to an end, and we now had to rely on our own resources.

Our personnel had undergone considerable alteration, for while several of our original members had dropped out, we had joined forces with Dr. Hector Munro's Ambulance Corps, and four of their doctors had joined our medical staff. Dr. Munro and his party had worked in connection with the hospitals of Ghent till the German advance forced both them and ourselves to retreat to Ostend. There we met and arranged to carry on our work together at Furnes. The arrangement was of the greatest possible advantage to both of us, for it gave us the service of their splendid fleet of ambulances, and it gave them a base to which to bring their wounded. We were thus able to get the wounded into hospital in an unusually short space of time, and to deal effectively with many cases which would otherwise have been hopeless. Smooth co-ordination with an ambulance party is, in fact, the first essential for the satisfactory working of an advanced hospital. If full use is to be made of its advantages, the wounded must be collected and brought in with the minimum of delay, whilst it must be possible to evacuate at once all who are fit to be moved back to the base. In both respects we were at Furnes exceptionally well placed.

We were established in a large straggling building of no attraction whatever except its cubic capacity. It was fairly new, and devoid of any of the interest of antiquity, but it presented none of the advantages of modern architecture. In fact, it was extremely ugly and extremely inconvenient, but it was large. Two of the largest classrooms and the refectory were converted into wards. At first the question of beds was a serious difficulty, but by the kind intervention of the Queen we were able to collect a number from houses in the town, whilst Her Majesty herself gave us twenty first-class beds with box-spring mattresses. Later on we got our supplies from England, and we could then find beds for a hundred patients. Even then we were not at the end of our capacity, for we had two empty classrooms, the floors of which we covered with straw, on which another fifty patients could lie in comfort until we could find better accommodation for them. We could not, of course, have fires in these rooms, as it would have been dangerous, but we warmed them by the simple plan of filling them with patients and shutting all the windows and doors. For the first few nights, as a matter of fact, we had to sleep in these rooms on straw ourselves, and in the greatest luxury. No one who has slept all his life in a bed would ever realize how comfortable straw is, and for picturesqueness has it an equal? I went into the Straw Ward on my round one wild and stormy night. Outside the wind was raging and the rain fell in torrents, and it was so dark that one had to feel for the door. Inside a dozen men lay covered up with blankets on a thick bed of straw, most of them fast asleep, while beside one knelt a nurse with a stable lantern, holding a cup to his lips. It was a picture that an artist might have come far to see—the wounded soldiers in their heavy coats, covered by the brown blankets; the nurse in her blue uniform and her white cap, the stable lantern throwing flickering shadows on the walls. It was something more than art, and as I glanced up at the crucifix hanging on the wall I felt that the picture was complete.

Above the two larger wards was a huge dormitory, divided up by wooden partitions into some sixty cubicles, which provided sleeping accommodation for the bulk of our staff. They were arranged in four ranks, with passages between and washing arrangements in the passages, and the cubicles themselves were large and comfortable. It was really quite well planned, and was most useful to us, though ventilation had evidently not appealed to its architect. Two rows were reserved for the nurses, and in the others slept our chauffeurs and stretcher-bearers, with a few of the priests. Our friends were at first much shocked at the idea of this mixed crowd, but as a matter of fact it worked very well, and there was very little to grumble at. The only real disadvantage was the noise made by early risers in the morning, convincing us more than ever of the essential selfishness of the early bird. A few of us occupied separate rooms over in the wing which the priests had for the most part reserved for themselves, and these we used in the daytime as our offices.

But the real sights of our establishment were our kitchen and our chef; we might almost have been an Oxford college. Maurice had come to us in quite a romantic way. One night we took in a soldier with a bullet wound of the throat. For some days he was pretty bad, but he won all our hearts by his cheerfulness and pluck. When at last he improved sufficiently to be able to speak, he told us that he was the assistant chef at the Hôtel Métropole in Brussels. We decided that he ought to be kept in a warm, moist atmosphere for a long time, and he was installed in the kitchen. He was a genius at making miracles out of nothing, and his soups made out of bacon rind and old bones, followed by entrées constructed from bully beef, were a dream. He was assisted by the nuns from Louvain who had accompanied us to Poperinghe, and who now worked for us on the sole condition that we should not desert them. They were very picturesque working in the kitchen in their black cloaks and coifs. At meal-times the

MAURICE.

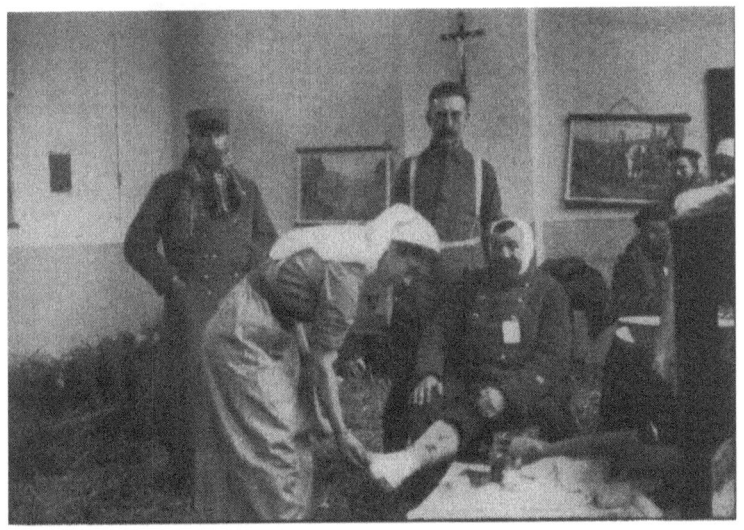

A STRAW WARD. FURNES.

scene was a most animated one, for, as we had no one to wait on us, we all came in one after the other, plate in hand, while Maurice stood with his ladle and presided over the ceremonies, with a cheery word for everyone, assisted by the silent nuns.

The getting of supplies became at times a very serious question. Needless to say, Furnes was destitute of anything to eat, drink, burn, or wear, and Dunkirk was soon in a similar case. We had to get most of our provisions over from England, and our milk came every morning on the Government transport, from Aylesbury. For some weeks we were very hard up, but the officer in charge of the naval stores at Dunkirk was very good to us, and supplied us with bully beef, condensed milk, cheese, soap, and many other luxuries till we could get further supplies from home. We used a considerable quantity of coal, and on one occasion we were faced by the prospect of an early famine, for Furnes and Dunkirk were empty. But nothing was ever too great a strain for the resources of our housekeeper. She discovered that there was a coal-heap at Ramscapelle, five miles away, and in a few hours an order had been obtained from the Juge d'Instruction empowering us to take the coal if we could get it, and the loan of a Government lorry had been coaxed out of the

War Lords. The only difficulty was that for the moment the Germans were shelling the place, and it was too dangerous to go near even for coal; so the expedition had to be postponed until they desisted. It seemed to me the most original method of filling one's coal-cellar of which I had ever heard. And it was typical of a large number of our arrangements. There is something of the Oriental about the Belgians and the French. If we wanted any special favour, the very last thing we thought of doing was to go and ask for it. It was not that they were not willing to give us what we asked for, but they did not understand that method of approach. What we did was to go to breakfast with the Juge, or to lunch with the Minister, or to invite the Colonel to dinner. In the course of conversation the subject would be brought up in some indirect way till the interest of the great man had been gained; then everything was easy. And surely there is something very attractive about a system where everything is done as an act of friendship, and not as the soulless reflex of some official machine. It is easier to drink red wine than to eat red tape, and not nearly so wearing to one's digestion.

As we were fifteen miles from Dunkirk, and as everything had to be brought out from there, transport was a serious problem. Every morning one of our lorries started for our seaport soon after nine, carrying the hospital mailbag and as many messages as a village carrier. The life of the driver was far more exciting than his occupation would suggest, and it was always a moot point whether or not he would succeed in getting back the same night. The road was of the usual Belgian type, with a paved causeway in the middle just capable of allowing two motors to pass, and on each side was a morass, flanked on the right by a canal and on the left by a field. The slightest deviation from the greasy cobbles landed the car in the mud, with quite a chance of a plunge into the canal. A constant stream of heavy army lorries tore along the road at thirty or more miles an hour, and as a rule absolutely refused to give way. It took a steady nerve to face them, encouraged as one was by numbers of derelicts in the field on the one side and half in the canal on the other. On one bridge a car hung for some days between heaven and earth, its front wheels caught over the parapet, and the car hanging from them over the canal—a heartening sight for a nervous driver. It was rarely that our lorry returned without some tale of adventure. The daily round, the common task, gave quite enough occupation to *one* member of the community.

XVIII
WORK AT FURNES

OUR work at Furnes differed in many ways from that at Antwerp. All its conditions were rougher, and, as we had to deal with a number of patients out of all proportion to our size, it was impossible to keep any but a few special cases for any length of time. We admitted none but the most serious cases, such as would be instantly admitted to any London hospital, and when I mention that in five weeks we had just a thousand cases in our hundred beds, the pressure at which the work was carried on will be realized. There is no hospital in England, with ten times the number of beds, that has ever admitted to its wards anything like this number of serious surgical cases. We were essentially a clearing hospital, with this important proviso, that we could, when it was required, carry out at once the heaviest operative work, and retain special cases as long as we thought fit. Our object was always to get each patient into such a condition that he could be transferred back to the base without injury to his chances of recovery, and

WORK AT FURNES

without undue pain, and I believe we saved the life of many a patient by giving him a night's rest in the Straw Ward, and sending him on next day with his wound properly dressed and supported. The cases themselves were of a far more severe type than those we had at Antwerp. There, indeed, I was astonished at the small amount of injury that had in many cases resulted from both shrapnel and bullet wounds, and it was certainly worthy of note that we had never once in our work there had to perform an amputation. At Furnes, we drew our patients from the line between Nieuport and Dixmude, where the fighting was for the most part at close range and of a most murderous nature. There were no forts, and the soldiers had little or no protection from the hail of high-explosive shells which the enemy poured upon them. In Nieuport and Dixmude themselves the fighting was frequently from house to house, the most deadly form of fighting known. The wounds we had to treat were correspondingly severe—limbs sometimes almost completely torn off, terrible wounds of the skull, and bullet wounds where large masses of the tissues had been completely torn away. It was difficult to see how human beings could survive such awful injuries, and, indeed, our death-roll was a long one. Added to this, the men had been working in the wet and the mud for weeks past. Their clothes were stiff with it, and such a thing as a clean wound was not to be thought of. Simple cases at Antwerp were here tedious and dangerous, and they required all the resources of nursing and of surgery that we could bring to bear upon them. Still, it was extraordinary what good results followed on common-sense lines of treatment, and we soon learnt to give up no case as hopeless. But each involved a great amount of work, first in operating and trying to reduce chaos to reason, and then in dressing and nursing. For everyone all round —surgeons, dressers, and nurses—it was real hard physical labour.

Our rapid turnover of patients involved a large amount of manual labour in stretcher work, clearing up wards, and so on, but all this was done for us by our *brancardiers*, or stretcher-bearers. These were Belgians who for one reason or another could not serve with the army, and who were therefore utilized by the Government for purposes such as these. We had some eight of them attached to our hospital, and they were of the greatest use to us, acting as hospital orderlies. They were mostly educated men — schoolmasters and University teachers—but they were quite ready to do any work we might require at any hour of the day or night. They carried the patients to the theatre

WORK AT FURNES 159

and to the wards, they cleaned the stretchers—a very difficult and unpleasant job—they tidied up the wards and scrubbed the floors, and they carried away all the soiled dressings and burned them. They were a fine set of men, and I do not know what we should have done without them.

Work began at an early hour, for every case in the hospital required dressing, and, as we never knew what we should have to deal with at night, we always tried to get through the routine before lunch. At ten o'clock Colonel Maestrio arrived, with two of his medical officers, and made a complete round of the hospital with the surgeons in charge of the various cases. They took the greatest interest in the patients, and in our attempts to cure them. They would constantly spend an hour with me in the operating theatre, and after any exceptional operation they would follow the progress of the patient with the keenest interest. Many of the cases with which we had to deal required a certain amount of ingenuity in the reconstruction of what had been destroyed, so that surgery had often to be on rather original lines. What interested them most was the fixation of fractures by means of steel plates, which we adopted in all our serious cases. Apparently the method is very little used abroad, and as an operation it is distinctly spectacular, for in a few minutes a shapeless mass which the patient cannot bear to be touched is transformed into a limb almost as strong as the other, which can be moved about in any direction without fear of breaking, and, when the patient recovers consciousness, almost without discomfort. We almost always had an interested audience, professional, clerical, or lay, for the chauffeurs found much amusement in these feats of engineering.

In the afternoon we almost always had some distinguished visitor to entertain, and it is one of my chief regrets that we never kept a visitors' book. Its pages would one day have been of the greatest interest. Twice every week the Queen of the Belgians came round our wards. She came quite simply, with one of her ladies and one of the Belgian medical officers, and no one could possibly have taken a deeper interest in the patients. Her father studied medicine as a hobby, and had, indeed, become a very distinguished physician, and she herself has had considerable training in medicine, so that her interest was a great deal more than that of an ordinary lay visitor. She was quite able to criticize and to appreciate details of nursing and of treatment. She always spoke to every patient, and she had a kind word for every one of them, Belgian, French, or even German, for we had a few Germans. There was

WORK AT FURNES

something deeply touching in the scene. The dimly lit ward, with its crude furniture, the slim figure in black, bending in compassion over the rough fellows who would gladly have given their lives for her, and who now lay wounded in the cause in which she herself had suffered. The Germans may destroy Belgium, but they will never destroy the kingdom of its Queen. Sometimes the King came to see his soldiers—a tall, silent man, with the face of one who has suffered much, and as simple, as gentle, and as kindly as his Queen. It was good to see the faces light up as he entered a ward, to see heads painfully raised to gaze after no splendid uniform, but a man.

One of our most distinguished and most welcome visitors was Madame Curie, the discoverer of radium. She brought her large X-ray equipment to Furnes for work amongst the wounded, and we persuaded her to stay with us for a week. One of our storerooms was rapidly fitted up as an impromptu radiographic department, the windows painted over and covered with thick paper, a stove introduced, and a dark-room contrived with the aid of a cupboard and two curtains. Electric current was obtained from a dynamo bolted on to the step of a twenty-horse-power car, and driven by a belt from the flywheel of the engine. The car stood out in the courtyard and snorted away, whilst we worked in the storeroom alongside. The coil and mercury break were combined in one piece, and the whole apparatus was skilfully contrived with a view to portability. Madame Curie was an indefatigable worker, and in a very short time had taken radiographs of all the cases which we could place at her disposal, and, indeed, we ransacked all the hospitals in Furnes, for when they heard of her arrival, they were only too glad to make use of the opportunity. Mademoiselle Curie developed the plates, and between them they produced photographs of the greatest utility to us. Considering its obvious utility, whether in war or in civil practice, it has always been a source of wonder to me that there is no such thing as a car designed and built with a view to radiography. Perhaps it exists, but if so, I have never met it. It only means the building into the frame of a suitable dynamo, and the provision of means for storing the rest of the equipment. It would place an X-ray equipment at the disposal of every cottage hospital, or even of a country-house, and it would place the cottage hospital, not to mention the country-house, at the disposal of the enterprising radiographer.

As soon as our patients could be moved, we had to send them on to their base hospitals—the Belgians to Calais and the French to Dunkirk.

MADAME CURIE (CENTRE).

WORK AT FURNES

From Calais the Belgians were brought over the Channel, and distributed all over England and Scotland. I had a postcard from one of them from Perth. The French were taken on in hospital ships to Cherbourg and other seaports along the coast. From Furnes they were all carried in hospital trains, and the scene at the station when a large batch of wounded was going off was most interesting. Only the worst cases were ever brought to our hospital; all the others were taken straight to the station, and waited there until a train was ready to take them on. Often they would be there for twelve hours, or even twenty-four, before they could be got on, and the train itself would be constantly shunted to let troops and ammunition go by, and might take twelve hours to reach its destination. There were no proper arrangements for the feeding of these men, all of whom were more or less badly wounded; and at first, when we heard at the hospital that a train was about to be made up, we took down all the soup and coffee we could manage to spare in big pails and jugs. But this was a mere makeshift, and was superseded very soon by a more up-to-date arrangement. A proper soup-kitchen was established at the station, with huge boilers full of soup and coffee always ready, and after that it was never necessary for a wounded soldier to leave Furnes hungry. All this was due to the energy and resource of Miss Macnaughtan, the authoress, who took it up as her special charge. She had a little passage screened off, and in this were fitted up boilers for coffee and soup, tables for cutting up meat and vegetables, and even a machine for cutting up the bread. It was all most beautifully arranged, and here she worked all day long, preparing for the inevitable crowd of wounded which the night would bring. How it was all managed was a mystery to me, for there was not enough food in Furnes to feed a tame cat, let alone a trainload of famished soldiers, and I am looking anxiously for her next book in the hopes of finding the solution.

The trains themselves were well equipped, though nothing to the hospital trains of England. The more severe cases were carried in long cars on a double row of stretchers, and they looked very comfortable on a cold night, with their oil-lamps and a coke stove in the centre of each car. A stretcher is, perhaps, not exactly a bed of roses for a wounded man, but when one considers what pain is involved in moving a man who is badly wounded, there is obviously a great advantage in placing him on a stretcher once for all on the battle-field, and never moving him again until he can be actually placed in bed in a hospital. On the train the men were looked after by the priests, splendid fellows who never seemed tired of doing all they could for the soldiers. One found the Belgian priest everywhere—in the trenches, in the hospitals, and in the trains—unobtrusive, always cheerful, always ready to help. From the brave Archbishop Mercier to the humblest village curé, regardless of their comfort and careless of their lives, they have stood by their people in the hour of their trial. May their honour be great in the hour of Belgium's triumph!

XIX

FURNES—THE TOWN

LIKE so many of the cities of Belgium, Furnes is a town of the past. To stand in the great square, surrounded by buildings which would delight the heart of any artist, is to travel back through three centuries of time. Spain and the Renaissance surround us, and we look instinctively towards the Pavillon for the soldiers of Philip, or glance with apprehension at the door of the Palais de Justice for the sinister form of Peter Titelmann the Inquisitor. Around this very square marched the procession of the Holy Office, in all the insolent blasphemy of its power, and on these very stones were kindled the flames that were to destroy its victims. But all these have gone; the priest and his victim, the swaggering bravo and the King he served, have gone to their account, and Furnes is left, the record of a time when men built temples like angels and worshipped in them like devils.

The immense square, with the beautiful public buildings which surround it, speaks of a time

St. Walburga, Furnes.

when Furnes was an important town. As early as the year 850 it is said that Baldwin of the Iron Arm, the first of the great Counts of Flanders, had established a fortress here to withstand the invasion of the Normans. After that Furnes appears repeatedly with varying fortunes in the turbulent history of the Middle Ages, until in the thirteenth century it was razed to the ground by Robert of Artois. In the next three hundred years, however, it must have entirely recovered its position, for in the days of the Spanish Fury it was one of the headquarters of the Inquisition and of the Spanish Army, and there is no town in Belgium upon which the Spanish occupation has left a greater mark. Since then, of no commercial or political importance, it has lived the life of a dull country town, and tradition says that there is plenty of solid wealth stored by its thrifty inhabitants behind the plain house-fronts which line its quiet streets.

From the centre of the square one can see all that there is to be seen of Furnes. The four sides are lined by beautiful old houses whose decorated fronts and elaborate gables tell of the Renaissance and of Spanish days. Behind the low red roofs tower the churches of St. Walburga and St. Nicholas, dwarfing the houses which nestle at their base. In the corners of the square are public buildings, small when compared with those of Bruges and Ypres, but unsurpassed in exquisite detail of design. Behind one corner rises the tall belfry without which no Flemish town would be complete. On an autumn evening when the sun is setting, when the red roofs glow with a deeper crimson, and the tall churches catch the sun's last rays on their old brick walls, there can be few more perfect pictures than the square of Furnes.

The two oldest buildings in the square stand at the ends of the eastern side. At the north end is the Pavillon des Officiers espagnols, once the Town Hall, and, in the days of the Spanish occupation, the headquarters of the army for the district. It is an old Flemish building, solidly built, with high-pitched roof, and windows framed in ornamental stonework, ending in a big square tower with battlements and little turrets at its corners. A short outside staircase leads up to the entrance. The whole building gives the impression that in the days when it was built the Town Hall was also the Fortress, and that the mayor had duties more strenuous than the eating of dinners. At the other end of the eastern side stands the old Halle aux Vins, where the night-watchmen had their quarters, a fine old gabled house with a loggia reached by a flight of steps

FURNES—THE TOWN

in the centre, a row of plain stone columns supporting the floors above.

Directly opposite is the north-west corner of the square, with the Palais de Justice on the right and the Hôtel de Ville on the left. Both date from the Spanish occupation, but they are very different in their style of architecture. The first is classical and severe, the second has all the warmth of the Renaissance. The Hôtel de Ville is an elaborately decorated building, with two exquisite gables and a steep roof surmounted by a little octagonal tower. The loggia below, standing out from the building and supporting a balcony above, is perhaps its most charming feature, both for the beauty of its proportions and the delicacy of its carved stone balustrades. Inside, the rooms are as they were three hundred years ago, and the wonderful hangings of Cordova leather in the council chamber are still intact. Beside the Hôtel de Ville the straight lines of the Palais de Justice, with its pillars and its high narrow windows, form a striking contrast. It was here, in the large room on the first floor, that the Inquisition held its awful court, and here were the instruments of torture with which it sought to enforce its will. Behind the Palais rises the tall belfry, a big square tower from which springs an octagonal turret carrying an elaborate campanile. There is a quaint survival on this belfry, for upon it the town crier has a little hut. He is a cobbler, and from below one can hear the tap-tap of his hammer as he plies his trade. But at night he calls out the hours to the town below, together with any information of interest, concluding with the assurance that he and his wife are in good health. The office has descended from father to son from the earliest days of the history of Furnes, and its holder has always been a cobbler. Till early in last November the record was unbroken, but, alas! the fear of German shells was too much for the cobbler, and he is gone.

Furnes is a town of contrasts, and though both its churches were built by the wonderful architects of the fourteenth century, there could hardly be two buildings more diverse. Behind the line of red roofs on the east of the square rises the rugged tower of St. Nicholas, a great square mass of old and weather-beaten brick, unfinished like so many of the Belgian towers, but rough, massive, and grand, like some rude giant. On the north, behind the Palais de Justice and the belfry, stands St. Walburga, with the delicate tracery of her flying buttresses and her spire fine as a needle. There is something fitting in the rugged simplicity which commemorates the grand old Bishop, and in the exquisite fragility of the shrine of the virgin saint. The double flying buttresses of St. Walburga, intersecting in mid-air, and apparently defying the laws of gravity, are as delicate a dream as the mind of architect could conceive, and they give to the whole an airy grace which cannot be described. The church was planned six hundred years ago on a gigantic scale, in the days when men built for the worship of God and not for the accommodation of an audience, and for six hundred years the choir stood alone as a challenge to future generations to complete what had been so gloriously begun. Only seven years ago the transept was added, and to the credit of its builders it is worthy to stand beside the choir. One wonders how many hundred years may have passed before the vision of the first great architect is complete. It is built for the most part of red brick, the rich red brick of Belgium, which grows only more mellow with age. Inside, the tall pillars of a dark grey stone support at a great height a finely groined roof of the same red brick, lit by a clerestory so open that one wonders how it can carry the weight of the roof above. The tall windows of the transept, reaching almost from the floor to the roof, with their delicate tracery, carry on the same effect of airiness, while their light is softened by the really beautiful stained glass which they frame. The richly carved choir-stalls of dark mahogany and the fine organ furnish an interior of which any town in England might well be proud. And all this magnificence is in a little Flemish town of some six thousand inhabitants.

One is brought suddenly face to face with the tremendous difference which exists between the Protestant and the Catholic conception of what a church is and what it is for. To the one it is a place where men meet for mutual support and instruction, for united worship; to the other it is a place where men meet God. To the one some organized service is necessary; the other only requires the stones on which to kneel. The one will only go to church—in fact, he will only find his church open at certain appointed times; for the other it is only closed with darkness. Of course, I am using the words Protestant and Catholic to indicate broad conceptions of religion, and not as defining definite bodies of men; but even of those who call themselves by these names what I have said is largely true. And this difference in conception is reflected in the churches which they build. For the one a simple building will suffice which will seat in comfort those who may come; the other, though he alone should ever enter it, will raise to heaven the mightiest temple which mortal hands can frame.

Furnes still carries on a tradition of medieval times — the strange procession which passes through its streets and across the great square on the last Sunday in July. Its origin, in the twelfth century, is unknown, though many legends are woven around it. It is a long procession, in which are represented many of the episodes in the story of the Christ, some in sculptured groups of figures, some by living actors. Before each group walks a penitent, barefoot and heavily veiled in black gown and hood, carrying an inscription to explain the group which follows. Abraham appears with Isaac, Moses with the serpent, Joseph and Mary, the Magi, and the flight into Egypt. Then come incidents from the life of Jesus, and the great tragedy of its close. The Host and its attendant priests conclude the procession. It is all very primitive and bizarre, but behind it there is a note of reality by which one cannot but be moved. For the figures concealed beneath the black hoods and dragging along the heavy wooden crosses are not actors; they are men and women who have come, many of them, long distances to Furnes, in the hope that by this penance they may obtain the forgiveness they desire.

XX
A JOURNEY

THE hospital had already been established in Furnes for ten days, and even in that time we had once had to escape to Poperinghe before the German advance, when, after a short visit to England, I left London to rejoin my friends on the last Friday in October. Crossing to the Continent is not at any time pleasant, and the addition of submarines and mines scarcely adds to its charms. But Government had certainly done their best to make it attractive, for when we arrived at Dover on Friday night we found a comfortable boat waiting to take us over in the morning. We spent the night soundly asleep in her cabins, without the anxiety of feeling that we might miss her if we did not get up in time, and after an excellent breakfast we felt ready for anything. We were late in starting, for the Anglo-Belgian Ambulance Corps was going over, and their ambulances had to be got on board. We watched them being neatly picked up in the slings and planted side by side on deck. At half-past eight they were all on board, and we started off.

There was a moderate sea running, but our three screws made light work of it, and in an hour we were half-way over to our destination, Dunkirk. We were sitting in our cabin talking when suddenly the engines stopped, and there was considerable commotion on deck. We looked out to see what was the matter, and there met our eyes a sight which we are likely to remember—a huge man-of-war sinking. She was down by the stern, so far that every now and then the waves broke over her, and it was evident that she would soon go under. A submarine had attacked her an hour before, and struck her with two torpedoes. The first destroyed her screws, and she was then an easy prey; the second entered her saloon in the stern. She was the *Hermes*, an old vessel, and of no great value at the present day, but it was tragic to see a great cruiser expiring, stabbed in the dark. Thanks to her buoyancy, she was only sinking slowly, and there was ample time for the whole of her crew to escape. Very different would be the fate of an unarmed vessel, for the explosion of a torpedo would probably blow such a large hole in the thin steel plates that she would go to the bottom like a stone. To torpedo a merchantman simply means the cold-blooded murder of the crew, for their chances of escape would be almost negligible, whilst it is impossible to find words to describe the attempts which have been made to sink hospital ships. About the last there is a degree of callous inhumanity remarkable even for Germany, for how could doctors and nurses make any efforts to save their own lives when it would be impossible for them to do anything to all at save the lives of their patients ? And yet these things are not the unconsidered acts of a moment; they are all part of the campaign of frightfulness which has been so carefully planned for years, the consummation of the doctrines which learned professors have proclaimed for so long and with such astonishing success.

The order was given for our boats to be lowered, and down they went all six of them, manned partly by the crew and partly by the Ambulance Corps. We were surrounded by torpedo-boats, British and French, and most of the crew of the *Hermes* had already been transferred to them. A few minutes later there was a cheer, and we saw the Captain step down into one of the boats, the last man to leave his ship. Our boats had picked up twenty or so of the men, and the problem now was to get them on board again. A moderate sea was running, but it required all the skill of our sailors to haul them up without mishap. Standing by as we were, the ship rolled considerably, and several times one of the boats was within an ace of being broken up against her side. To get a boat out from a big liner in a heavy sea must be an almost miraculous feat, whilst to get her back again must be a sheer impossibility. As it was, it took us at least an hour to get those six boats on board. All this time four torpedo-boats were racing in circles round and round us, on the lookout for the submarine, and ready to cut it down if it should appear. Indeed, a report went round that a torpedo was actually fired at us, but passed underneath the ship on account of her shallow draught. Standing at rest, we would have been an easy target, and but for our friends the torpedo-boats we should very likely have been attacked. It is not a good plan to hang about in the Channel just now.

Meanwhile the *Hermes* was steadily sinking. By the time all her crew were off her stern was awash, and in another half-hour she had a very marked list to port. She slowly, almost imperceptibly, listed more and more, and then the end came with startling suddenness. With a slow and gentle roll she heeled over till she was completely on her side and her great funnels under water; she remained there for a moment, and then slowly turned turtle and gradually sank stern first. For a long time about twenty feet of her nose remained above water, then this slowly sank and disappeared. It was all so quiet that it seemed like some queer dream. The fires must have been drawn with great promptness, for there was no explosion as her funnels went under, though we were standing some way off to be clear of flying fragments. She had been stabbed in the dark, and she passed away without a murmur.

There is something very moving in the end of a great vessel. It is so hard to believe that a thing of such vast bulk, and with organs of such terrific power, should be so utterly helpless because of a mere hole in her side. It is like watching the death of a god. We make such a turmoil about the end of our puny lives, and that great giant slides away into darkness without a murmur. Ah, but you will say, a man is of far more value than a ship. Is he? Is any single man in this world worth as much as the *Titanic?* And if so, how? He can make wealth, but so could she. He could bring happiness to others, and so could she. I have yet to find any ground on which any man can be put up in competition with that vessel in sheer worth to the world, and I am not speaking in any low sense of values. For I suppose the greatest man who ever lived might feel that his life was well spent if he had brought two continents nearer together. It was for that that

A JOURNEY 179

she was created. The hard fact is that there are very few indeed of us, in spite of all the noise we make, who are worth to the world a thousand pounds, and if she could sell the bulk of us for that she would be positively drunk with fortune.

But, you will say, a ship has no soul. Are you quite so sure about that? Most people will maintain that their bodies contain a soul, and then they proceed to build up these same bodies with bread and bacon, and even beer, and in the end they possess bodies constructed without any shadow of doubt out of these ingredients. And if ten thousand men have toiled night and day, in blazing furnace and in dark mine, to build a mighty vessel, at the cost of years of labour, at the cost of pain and death, is not that vessel a part of them as much as their poor bodies, and do not their souls live in it as much as in their flesh and blood? We speak of the resurrection of the Body, and superior people smile at an idea so out-of-date and unscientific. To me the body is not mere flesh and blood, it is the whole complex of all that a man has thought and lived and done, and when it arises there will arise with it all that he has toiled for on earth, all that he has gained, and all that he has created by the sweat of his brow and the hunger of his soul. The world is not the dust-heap of the centuries, but only their storehouse.

It was late when we reached Furnes after a freezing drive in the dark, but all our thoughts were overshadowed by the tragedy we had seen. We felt that we had been present at the burial of a god.

XXI

THE AMBULANCE CORPS

ONE of the most difficult problems for a medical service in war is the recovery of the wounded from the field of battle and their carriage back to hospital. In the old days men fought out a battle in a few hours, and the field at the end of the day was left to the conqueror. Then the doctors could go forward and attend to the wounded on the spot without any special danger to themselves. A man might lie out all night, but he would be certain to be picked up next day. But in this war everything is changed. It is one continuous siege, with the result that the removal of the wounded is a matter of extraordinary difficulty and danger. I have met with one officer who has been in a trench out at the extreme front for two and a half months. During the whole of that time he has never seen a German, and the nearest German trench is just one hundred yards away! Shell and shot have been pouring over his head all that time, and to raise one's head above the ground would be to court instant death.

Between the trenches the ground is a quagmire, and any advance by either side is out of the question. But a time will come when the ground is just solid enough for a man to stand, there will be a desperate struggle for a few yards of ground, again both sides will subside into new trenches; but now between those trenches will lie perhaps some hundreds of wounded, and how in the world are they to be got? This is the problem with which an ambulance is everywhere faced—the recovery of the wounded from disputed ground. It was to grapple with difficulties like these that the rules of the Geneva Convention were framed, so that men wearing a Red Cross on their arms might be able to go where no combatant of either side dare venture, and succour the wounded, whether they were friend or foe, in safety both for themselves and for the wounded. It is, after all, possible to fight as gentlemen.

Or at least it was until a few months ago. Since then we have had a demonstration of " scientific " war such as has never before been given to mankind. Now, to wear a Red Cross is simply to offer a better mark for the enemy's fire, and we only wore them in order that our own troops might know our business and make use of our aid. A hospital is a favourite mark for the German artillery, whilst the practice of painting

THE AMBULANCE CORPS 183

Red Crosses on the tops of ambulance cars is by many people considered unwise, as it invites any passing aeroplane to drop a bomb. But the Germans have carried their systematic contempt of the rules of war so far that it is now almost impossible for our own men to recognize their Red Crosses. Time after time their Red Cross cars have been used to conceal machine-guns, their flags have floated over batteries, and they have actually used stretchers to bring up ammunition to the trenches. Whilst I was at Furnes two German spies were working with an ambulance, in khaki uniforms, bringing in the wounded. They were at it for nearly a week before they were discovered, and then, by a ruse, they succeeded in driving straight through the Belgian lines and back to their own, Red Cross ambulance, khaki and all.

The problems, then, that have to be faced by an ambulance corps in the present war are fairly perplexing, and they demand a degree of resource and cool courage beyond the ordinary. That these qualities are possessed by the members of the ambulance corps of which Dr. Hector Munro and Lady Dorothie Feilding are the leading members is merely a matter of history. They have been in as many tight corners in the last few months as many an old and seasoned veteran, and they have invariably come out triumphant. They started in

Ghent under the Belgian Red Cross with a party of four surgeons, five women, and three men for the stretchers, and two chauffeurs to drive the two ambulances. Now they have grown into an organization which takes on a great part of the ambulance work of the Belgian Army. At Ghent they were attached to the big Red Cross hospital in the Flandria Palace Hotel, and at first it was dull, for most of the fighting was around Antwerp, and the wounded were taken there. We were in Antwerp just then, and it was by no means dull. We shared Alost and Termonde as a common hunting-ground, and we several times had a visit from Dr. Munro in the Boulevard Leopold. In fact, we were discussing the possibility of arranging to work together when the crash came and Antwerp fell.

For the next few days the ambulance corps had enough work and ran enough risks to satisfy even the members of that notorious organization. The Germans were coming on with great rapidity, and if there is one dangerous job, it is to pick up the wounded of a retreating army. But here the interest for an English ambulance was doubled, for the British Army was covering the retreat of the Belgians and the French. On Sunday, the 11th of October, they were asked to go out to Melle, four miles south-east of Ghent, to help with some

THE AMBULANCE CORPS 185

French wounded, and, after spending some time there, they met the British Staff, and were asked to help them in their retreat through Zwynarde, a town on the Scheldt about four miles south of Ghent and the same distance from Melle. It was a dangerous undertaking, as the intention was to blow up the bridge which crosses the Scheldt at Zwynarde and to fight a retreating battle covering the retirement of our allies. The bridge was to be blown up at ten o'clock that evening, and though it was only four miles away, it was already dark and a mist was rising from the river. The main roads were in the hands of the Germans, and there was nothing for it but to get across by a small side-road. They started off in the mist, and promptly lost their way. It is a pleasing situation to be lost in the dark somewhere very close to the enemy's lines when you know that the only available bridge is just going to be blown up. A thick mist had risen all around, and they were midway between two batteries—British and German—engaged in an artillery duel. The crash of the guns and the scream of the shells overhead filled the darkness with terror. But there was nothing for it but to go straight on, and though they must have gone right through the German lines and out again, they reached the bridge just ten minutes before it was blown into the air.

We all met at Ostend, and decided to join forces at Furnes, and it worked out as a splendid arrangement for both parties. Though our organizations remained entirely distinct, we worked together, and they had the advantage of a hospital to which they could always bring their patients, whilst we had the services of the smartest ambulance corps on the Continent. The qualities required for the satisfactory working of a hospital and the successful running of an ambulance are so distinct that I am sure that the ideal arrangement is to have two entirely distinct organizations working in harmony.

The position of an ambulance up at the front is always a delicate one, for as it moves about from place to place its members have opportunities of picking up information about the position and movements of the troops of a very confidential nature. It was therefore a great advantage to Dr. Munro when his party was joined by M. de Broqueville, the son of the Minister for War; for it meant that they would have full information as to where wounded were likely to require their help, and that they possessed the full confidence of the Belgian authorities. Their position and our own had been very greatly affected by the fortunes of the war, for the Belgian Croix Rouge and Army Medical Services were for the moment in

THE AMBULANCE CORPS 187

abeyance, and instead of obtaining from them the help which had hitherto been so generously given, we had now to undertake their work and to rely entirely on our own resources. We had not to wait long for an opportunity to show what we could do.

The Belgian Army, supported by a certain number of French troops, made its final stand on the line of the Yser, the little river which runs from Ypres through Dixmude and Nieuport to the sea. From this position they have never since been shaken, but they have never had to withstand more desperate attacks than those which took place in the end of October. The centre of these was Dixmude, and here the Germans threw against the little remnant of the Belgian Army forces which might have been expected to shatter it at a blow. Their efforts culminated in one of the fiercest and bloodiest engagements of the whole war, and at the height of the engagement word came that there were wounded in Dixmude, and that ambulances were urgently required to get them out. Getting wounded out of a town which is being shelled is not exactly a joke, and when the town is in rapid process of annihilation it almost becomes serious. But this was what the Corps had come out for, and two ambulances and an open car started off at once. As far as Oudecappelle the road was crowded with motor transport waggons carrying supplies of food and ammunition to the troops, but beyond that it was empty, unless one counts the shells which were falling on it in a steady hail. Every now and then a Jack Johnson would fall and leave a hole in which one could bury a motor, and, apart from the shells, the holes made driving risky. There was over a mile of the road in this unhealthy state, and entirely exposed to the enemy's guns, before any shelter could be obtained; but the wounded must be fetched, and the cars pushed on as fast as they dared to drive. They were suddenly pulled up by an appalling obstacle. A Belgian battery advancing along the road to the front only twenty minutes before had been struck by a big shell. Several of the gunners were horribly mangled; ten horses lay dead, most of them in fragments; the gun was wrecked, and all its equipment scattered about the road. It was some minutes before the remaining soldiers could clear the road sufficiently for the cars to pass.

Dixmude itself was a roaring furnace, and shells were pouring into it in all directions. Practically every house had been damaged, many were totally demolished, and many more were on fire. The wounded were in the Town Hall on the square, and shells were bursting all over it. The upper portion was completely destroyed, and the church close by was blazing furiously, and must have set fire to the Town Hall soon after. On the steps lay a dead Marine, and beside him stood a French surgeon, who greeted them warmly. The wounded were in a cellar, and if they were not got out soon, it was obvious that they would be burned alive. Inside the hall were piles of bicycles, loaves of bread, and dead soldiers, all in gruesome confusion. In the cellar dead and wounded were lying together. The wounded had all to be carried on stretchers, for everyone who could crawl had fled from that ghastly inferno, and only those who have shifted wounded on stretchers can appreciate the courage it requires to do it under shell fire. At last they were all packed into the ambulances, and even as they left the building with the last, a shell struck it overhead and demolished one of the walls. How they ever got out of Dixmude alive is beyond the ken of a mere mortal, but I suppose it was only another manifestation of the Star which shines so brightly over the fortunes of the Munro Ambulance.

How high is the appreciation of the Belgian Government for their work is shown in the fact that three of the lady members of the Corps have just been decorated with the Order of Leopold—one of the highest honours which Belgium has to confer. It is not every honour which is so well earned.

XXII

PERVYSE—THE TRENCHES

This is indeed the strangest of all wars, for it is fought in the dark. Eyes are used, but they are the eyes of an aeroplane overhead, or of a spy in the enemy's lines. The man who fights lives underground, or under water, and rarely sees his foe. There is something strangely terrible, something peculiarly inhuman, in the silent stealth of this war of the blind. The General sits in a quiet room far behind the lines, planning a battle he will never see. The gunner aims by level and compass with faultless precision, and hurls his awful engines of destruction to destroy ten miles away a house which is to him only a dot on a map. And the soldier sitting in his trench hears the shells whistling overhead and waits, knowing well that if he appeared for one instant above that rampart of earth he would be pierced by a dozen bullets from rifles which are out of his sight.

It is a war in the dark, and by far the most

important of its operations are carried on, its battles are fought, in the literal sense of the word, underground. Perhaps the next war will be fought not merely underground, but deep in the bowels of the earth, and victory will rest, not with the finest shots or the expert swordsmen, but with the men who can dig a tunnel most quickly. The trenches may be cut by some herculean plough, deep tunnels may be dug by great machines, and huge pumping engines may keep them dry. Our engineers have conquered the air, the water, and the land, but it is still with picks and spades that our soldiers dig themselves into safety.

At Furnes the nearest point to us of the fighting line was Pervyse, and as the Ambulance Corps had a dressing-station there, we often went out to see them and the soldiers in the trenches close by. But the Belgian line was most effectively protected by an agency far more powerful than any trench, for over miles and miles of land spread the floods with which the Belgians, by breaking down the dykes, had themselves flooded the country. The floods were a protection, but they were also a difficulty, since they made actual trenches an impossibility. No ordinary pumps could have kept them dry. So they had built huts of earth behind a thick earth bank, and partly sunk in the very low embankment, only two or three feet above the fields, on which the railway ran. They were roofed with boards covered again with earth and sods, and behind each was a little door by which one could crawl in. Inside, the floor was covered with a bed of straw, and a bucket with holes in its sides and full of red-hot coke did duty as a stove, while narrow loopholes served for ventilation and for light, and were to be used for firing from in the event of an attack. Of course the huts were very cramped, but they were at least warm, they gave protection from the weather, and above all they were safe. The men only occupied them as a matter of fact for short periods of one or two days at a time, a fresh guard coming out from Furnes to take their places.

These huts, and all covered trenches, are only safe from shrapnel exploding in the air or near by. No ordinary trench is safe from a shell falling upon it; but this, as a matter of fact, has scarcely ever happened. For shells are as a rule fired from some considerable distance, and in most cases the opposing lines of trenches are so close together that there would be great danger of sending a shell into the back of your own trench, the most deadly disaster that can happen. The trenches are often so close together that their occupants can talk to one another, and a considerable amount of camaraderie may spring up.

PERVYSE—THE TRENCHES

I know of one instance where a private arrangement was made that they would not shoot on either side. One day a man on our side was wounded, and there was great annoyance till a note was thrown across apologizing profusely, and explaining that it was done by a man in a trench behind who did not know of the compact! A few days later a message came to say that an important officer was coming to inspect the German trench, and that they would be obliged to fire, but that they would give due warning by three shots fired in quick succession. The shots were fired, and our men lay low, under a storm of bullets, till firing ceased, and another message arrived to say that the danger was past. We really are queer animals!

Behind the trenches at Pervyse the fields were positively riddled with shot-holes. In one space, not more than twenty yards square, we counted the marks of over a hundred shells. The railway station was like a sieve, and most of the houses in the little town were absolutely destroyed. I do not believe that there was a house in the place which had not been hit, and the number of shells that must have rained on that small area would have sufficed not so many years ago for the siege of a large town. The church was destroyed beyond any possibility of repair. The roof was gone entirely, and large portions of the walls; a great piece of the tower had been blown clean out, and the tower itself was leaning dangerously. The bombardment of the church must have been terrific, for even the heavy pillars of the aisle had been snapped across. Of the altar only the solid stones remained, surrounded by fragments of what had once been the stained glass of the apse, and the twisted remains of the great brass candlesticks which had stood beside the altar. Only a few weeks ago this was an old parish church of singular beauty. Now even the graves in the churchyard have been torn open by the shells. These few battered walls, these heaps of stone and brick, are all that remain of a prosperous village and its ancient church.

The dressing station of the Ambulance Corps was one of their most daring and successful ventures. At first it was placed close to the trenches and just behind the railway station, in the house of the village chemist. At least there were evidences in the existence of portions of walls, roof, and floors that it had once been a house, and the chemist had left a few bottles behind to indicate his trade. But I do not think that anyone but a member of the Corps would have ever thought of living there. There was plenty of ventilation, of course, since there were no windows

PERVYSE.

YPRES.

left, part of the roof had gone, and the walls were riddled with holes through which shells had passed clean across the building. It could hardly be described as a desirable residence, but it had one incomparable advantage: it possessed a cellar. A couple of mattresses and a few blankets converted it into a palace, whilst the limits of luxury were reached when there arrived a new full-sized enamelled bath which one of the soldiers had discovered and hastened to present as a mark of gratitude. There was no water-supply, of course, and I do not think that there was a plug, but those were mere trifles. How such a white elephant ever found its way to Pervyse none of us will ever know. I do not believe that there was another for twenty miles around.

In this strange residence—it could hardly be called a house—lived two of the lady members of the Corps. They were relieved from time to time, two others coming out to take their places, and every day they had visits from the ambulances which came out to pick up the wounded. A room on the ground floor was used during the day, partly as a living-room, partly as a surgery, and here were brought any soldiers wounded in this part of the lines. At night they retired to the cellar, as the house itself was far too dangerous. The Germans shelled Pervyse almost every night, and sometimes in the day as well, and this particular house was the most exposed of any in the town. But shells were not the only trouble, and when a few weeks later the cellars were filled with water, it was evident that other quarters must be found.

Pervyse was of course entirely deserted by its inhabitants, but it could scarcely be called dull. We went out one afternoon to see what was going on, and found a party of the Corps at lunch. They seemed to be in particularly good spirits, and they told us that the house had just been struck by a shell, that the big Daimler ambulance had been standing outside, and that its bonnet had been riddled by the shrapnel bullets. We went outside to see for ourselves, and there we found a large hole in the side of the house, through which a shell had entered a room across the passage from that occupied by the Corps, who had fortunately chosen the lee-side. The big six-cylinder Daimler had been moved into a shed, and there it stood with twenty or more holes in its bonnet, but otherwise uninjured. By a stroke of luck the driver had gone inside the house for a moment or he would undoubtedly have been killed. It is fortunate that the Corps is possessed of such a keen sense of humour.

Shells may be amusing in the daytime, but they

are not a bit amusing at night. Only two women with real solid courage could have slept, night after night, in that empty house in a ruined and deserted village, with no sounds to be heard but the rain and the wind, the splutter of the mitrailleuse, and the shriek of shells. Courage is as infectious as fear, and I think that the soldiers, watching through the night in the trenches near by, must have blessed the women who were waiting there to help them, and must have felt braver men for their presence.

Pervyse was protected by a wide screen of flood, and across this there was one way only—a slightly raised road going straight across six miles of water. No advance by either side was possible, for the road was swept by mitrailleuses, and to advance down it would have meant certain death. Half a mile down the road was a farmhouse held by a Belgian outpost, and beyond this, and perhaps half a mile away from it, were two other farms occupied by the Germans. We could see them moving amongst the trees. That piece of road between Pervyse and the Belgian farm was the scene of one of the very few lapses of the Germans into humanity.

It was known one morning in the trenches at Pervyse that several of their comrades in the farm had been injured in an outpost engagement. It was, however, impossible to reach them before nightfall as the road was swept by the German guns. Two Belgian priests, taking their lives in their hands, walked out to the farm, but they found that the wounded were beyond their powers of carriage. Nothing daunted, they went on to one of the German farms and asked for help, and a few minutes later the astounded Belgians saw a little procession coming up the road. In front walked the two priests, and behind them came four wounded Belgians, lying on stretchers carried by German soldiers. They came right into the lines, and they had a royal welcome. They all shook hands, and the little party of Germans walked back down the road amid the cheers of their opponents.

The spirit of chivalry is not dead in Germany; it is only stifled by her present rulers. Is it too much to hope that some day its voice may be heard and may command?

XXIII

YPRES

ONE morning early in December I was asked by Dr. Munro to run down with him in one of our motors to Ypres. A message had arrived saying that the town had been heavily shelled during the night, and that there were a number of children and of wounded there, who ought if possible to be removed to some less dangerous situation. So we started off to see what we could do for them. It was a dismal morning, and the rain was coming down in a steady drizzle which continued all day long, but fortunately we had a closed car, and we were protected from the elements. The road to Ypres is a broad avenue between long lines of tall trees, and to-day it was crowded with soldiers and transport motors. The French were moving up a large number of men to relieve and to support their lines between Dixmude and Ypres. Every little village seemed to be crowded with troops, for in this weather " the poorest village is better than the best bivouac," and the contrasts of the uniforms were very striking. Every type was represented—the smart French officer, the Zouave, the Turco, and the Arab, and one could not help wondering what the Senegalese and the Algerians thought of this soaking rain, or how they would fare in the rigours of a Belgian winter.

Like so many of the towns of Belgium, Ypres is a town of the past, and it is only in the light of its history that the meaning of its wonderful buildings can be realized, or an estimate formed of the vandalism of its destroyers. Its records date back to the year 900, and in the twelfth century it was already famous for its cloth. By the thirteenth century it was the richest and the most powerful city in Flanders, and four thousand looms gave occupation to its two hundred thousand inhabitants. These great commercial cities were also great military organizations, and there were few wars in the turbulence of the Middle Ages in which Ypres did not have a share. In fact, it was almost always engaged in fighting either England, or France, or one of the other Flemish towns.

After a century of wars, to which Ypres once contributed no fewer than five thousand troops, the town was besieged by the English, led by Henry Spencer, Bishop of Norwich, with the help of the burghers of Ghent and Bruges. The town was surrounded by earthen ramparts planted with thick hedges of thorn, and by wide ditches and wooden palisades, and these were held by some ten thousand men. They were attacked, in 1383, by seventeen thousand English and twenty thousand Flemish. For two months Ypres was defended against almost daily attacks in one of the fiercest and most bloody sieges in history. At last Spencer saw that it was impossible to take the town by assault, and in view of the advance of a large French army he withdrew. Ypres was saved, but its prosperity was gone, for the bulk of its population had fled. The suburbs, where large numbers of the weavers worked, had been destroyed by the besiegers and the looms had been burnt. The tide of trade turned to Bruges and Ghent, though they did not enjoy for long the prosperity they had stolen.

The commercial madness of the fourteenth century gave way to the religious madness of the sixteenth. Men's ideas were changing, and it is a very dangerous thing to change the ideas of men. For the momentum of the change is out of all proportion to its importance, and the barriers of human reason may melt before it. It is a mere matter of historical fact that no oppression has half the dangers of an obvious reform. At Ypres the Reformers were first in the field. They had swept through Flanders, destroying all the beauty and wealth that the piety of ages had accumulated, and here was rich plunder for these apostles of the ugly. There is real tragedy in the thought that the Reformer is sometimes sincere.

But at least the fanatics limited their fury to the symbols of religion. Philip of Spain could only be sated by flesh and blood, and for the next fifteen years Ypres was tossed to and fro in an orgy of persecution and war such as have rarely been waged even in the name of religion. At the end of that time only a miserable five thousand inhabitants remained within its broken ramparts.

With the seventeenth century commerce and religion made way for politics, and the wars of Louis XIV. fell heavily on Ypres. On four separate occasions the town was taken by the French, and the dismantled fortifications which still surround it were once an example of the genius of Vauban. Yet with all these wars—commercial, religious, political—with all the violence of its history, Ypres had kept intact the glorious monuments of the days of her greatness, and it has been left for the armies of Culture to destroy that which even the hand of Philip spared.

The centuries have handed down to us few buildings of such massive grandeur as the great Cloth Hall, a monument of the days when the Weavers of Ypres treated on equal terms with the Powers of England and of France. This huge

THE CLOTH HALL, YPRES, AFTER BOMBARDMENT.

fortress of the Guilds is about a hundred and fifty yards long. The ground floor was once an open loggia, but the spaces between its fifty pillars have been filled in. Above this are two rows of pointed windows, each exactly above an opening below. In the upper row every second window has been formed into a niche for the figure of some celebrity in the history of the town. A delicate turret rises at each end of the façade, and above it rose the high-pitched roof which was one of the most beautiful features of the building. In the centre is the great square tower, reaching to a height of more than two hundred feet, and ending in an elegant belfry, which rises between its four graceful turrets. The whole of this pile was finished in 1304; but in the seventeenth century there was added at its eastern end the Nieuwerck, an exquisite Renaissance structure supported entirely on a row of slim columns, with tiers of narrow oblong windows, and with elaborate gables of carved stone. The contrast between the strength and simplicity of the Gothic and the rich decoration of Spain is as delightful as it is bold. The upper part of this vast building formed one great hall, covered overhead by the towering roof. The walls were decorated by painted panels representing the history of the town, and so large were these that in one bay there was erected the entire front of an old wooden house which had been pulled down in the town, gable and all.

And all this is a heap of ruins. Whether any portion of it can ever be repaired I do not know, but the cost would be fabulous. The roof is entirely destroyed, and with it the whole of the great gallery and its paintings, for fire consumed what the shells had left. Only the bare stone walls remain, and as we stood among the pillars which had supported the floors above, it was difficult to realize that the heap of rubbish around us was all that was left of what had once been the envy of Europe. The only building which we have at all comparable to the Cloth Hall is the Palace of Westminster. If it were blasted by shells and gutted by fire, we might regret it, but what would be our feelings if it were the legacy of Edward the First, and had been handed down to us intact through six centuries ?

Behind the Cloth Hall stands the Church of St. Martin, once for two and a half centuries the Cathedral of Ypres. It was largely built at the same time as the Cloth Hall, and it is a glorious monument of the architecture of the thirteenth century. Perhaps its most beautiful features are the great square tower, the lofty and imposing nave, and the exquisite rose window in the south wall of the transept, which is said to be the finest in Belgium. The tower was surrounded with scaffolding, and around its base were piles of stone, for the church was being repaired when the war began. I wonder if it will ever be repaired now. The Germans had expended on its destruction many of their largest shells, and they had been very successful in their efforts. There were three huge holes in the roof of the choir where shells had entered, and in the centre of the transept was a pile of bricks and stone six feet high. Part of the tower had been shot away, and its stability was uncertain. The beautiful glass of the rose window had been utterly destroyed, and part of the tracery was broken. The old Parish Chapel on the south side of the nave had nothing left but the altar and four bare walls. The fine old roof and the great bronze screen which separated it from the nave had perished in the flames. The screen was lying in small fragments amongst the rubbish on the chapel floor, and at first I thought they were bits of rusty iron.

As I stood in the ruins of the Parish Chapel looking round on this amazing scene, there was a roar overhead, and one of the big 14-inch shells passed, to explode with a terrific crash amongst the houses a few hundred yards farther on. It was plain that the bombardment was beginning again, and that we must see to our business without any delay. Two more shells passed overhead as I came out of the church, with a roar very different from the soft whistle of a small shell. The destruction produced by one of these large shells is astonishing. One large house into which a shell had fallen in the previous night had simply crumpled up. Portions of the walls and a heap of bricks were all that was left, a bit of an iron bedstead and a fragment of staircase sticking out from the débris. The roof, the floors, and the greater part of the walls might never have existed. In the Place in front of the Cathedral were two holes where shells had fallen, and either of them would have comfortably held a motor-car.

The children were all together in a little street a quarter of a mile west of the Cathedral, just where the last three shells had fallen. Fortunately they had hurt no one, though one had passed clean through the upper stories of a house where there were several children being got ready by one of our party for removal. By good luck through some defect it did not explode, or the house would have been annihilated and everyone in it killed. Quite a collection of people had congregated in that little street, though why they considered it safer than the rest of the town I do not know. At first they were very unwilling to let any of the children go at all. But at last about twenty children were collected and were packed into ambulances. Some of them were without parents, and were being looked after by the neighbours, and the parents of some absolutely refused to leave. More children and a few adults to look after them were found later, and I think that in the end about a hundred were taken up to Furnes, to be sent on to Calais as refugees.

The children were as merry as crickets, and regarded it all as a huge joke; sitting in the ambulances, they looked for all the world like a school treat. But I have often wondered whether we were right to take them away or whether it would not have been better to have left them to take their chance. War is a very terrible thing, and the well-meant interference of the kind-hearted may do far more harm than good. What is going to happen to those children? I suppose that they are in some refugee home, to remain there till the war is over. And then? We did our best to identify them, but what are the chances that many of them will ever see their parents again? From what I have seen of these things I do not think that they are very large. Perhaps you will say that the parents ought to have gone with them. It is easy for the well-to-do to leave their homes and to settle again elsewhere; but the poorer a man is the less can he afford to leave what little he possesses. In their own town they might be in danger, but at least they had not lost their homes, and they possessed the surroundings without which their individual lives would be merged in the common ocean of misery. The problem of the civil population, and especially of the children, in time of war is entirely beyond the scope of individual effort. It is a matter with which only a Government or a very powerful organization can deal, and it is a matter in which Governments do not take a great deal of interest. Their hands are quite full enough in trying to defeat the enemy.

In all previous wars between civilized nations a certain regard has been paid to the safety of the civilian population, and especially of the women and children. But from the very first the German policy has been to utterly ignore the rights of non-combatants, tearing up the conventions which they themselves had signed for their protection. No Government could be expected to be prepared for such a total apostasy from the elementary principles of civilized society, or to anticipate methods at which a Zulu might blush. If they had done so, it should have been their first care to remove all non-combatants from the area of fighting, and to make provision for them elsewhere. It is unfair that a civilian should be left with the hopeless choice of leaving a child in a house where it may at any moment be killed by a shell or taking it away with a considerable probability that it will be a homeless orphan. For life is a matter of small moment; it is living that matters.

The problem of the children of Belgium will be one of the most serious to be faced when the war is over. There will be a great number of orphans, whilst many more will be simply lost. They must not be adopted in England, for to them Belgium will look for her future population. There could be few finer ways in which we could show our gratitude to the people of Belgium than by establishing colonies over there where they could be brought up in their own country, to be its future citizens. It would form a bond between the two countries such as no treaty could ever establish, and Belgium would never forget the country which had been the foster-mother of her children.

But Ypres gave us yet another example of German methods of war. On the western side of the town, some distance from the farthest houses, stood the Asylum. It was a fine building arranged in several wings, and at present it was being used for the accommodation of a few wounded, mostly women and children, and several old people of the workhouse infirmary type. It made a magnificent hospital, and as it was far away from the town and was not used for any but the purposes of a hospital, we considered that it was safe enough, and that it would be a pity to disturb the poor old people collected there. We might have known better. The very next night the Germans shelled it to pieces, and all those unfortunate creatures had to be removed in a hurry. There is a senseless barbarity about such an act which could only appeal to a Prussian.

XXIV

SOME CONCLUSIONS

To draw conclusions from a limited experience is a difficult matter, and the attempt holds many pitfalls for the unwary. Yet every experience must leave on the mind of any thinking man certain impressions, and the sum of these only he himself can give. To others he can give but blurred images of all he may have seen, distorted in the curving mirrors of his mind, but from these they can at least form some estimate of the truth of the conclusions he ventures to draw. For myself, these conclusions seem to fall naturally into three separate groups, for I have met the experiences of the past three months in three separate ways—as a surgeon, as a Briton, and as, I hope, a civilized man. It is from these three aspects that I shall try to sum up what I have seen.

As a surgeon it has been my good fortune to have charge of a hospital whose position was almost ideal. Always close to the front, we received our cases at the earliest possible moment, and could deal with them practically first hand. Every day I realized more strongly the advantages of such a hospital, and the importance for the wounded of the first surgical treatment they receive. Upon this may well depend the whole future course of the case. No wounded man should be sent on a long railway journey to the base until he has passed through the hands of a skilled surgeon, and has been got into such a condition that the journey does not involve undue risk. And no rough routine treatment will suffice. A surgeon is required who can deal with desperate emergencies and pull impossible cases out of the fire—a young man who does not believe in the impossible, and who can adapt himself to conditions of work that would make an older man shudder, and a man who will never believe what he is told until he has seen it for himself. For the conditions of work at the front are utterly different from those of civil practice, and it is impossible for any man after many years of regular routine to adapt himself to such changed environment. The long experience of the older man will be of far more use at the base, and he will have plenty of difficulties to contend with there.

I have often been told that there is no opening for skilled surgery at the front. In my opinion

SOME CONCLUSIONS 213

there is room for the highest skill that the profession can produce. It is absurd to say that the abdominal cases should be left to die or to recover as best they can, that one dare not touch a fractured femur because it is septic. To take up such an attitude is simply to admit that these cases are beyond the scope of present surgery. In a sense, perhaps, they are, but that is all the more reason why the scope of surgery should be enlarged, and not that these cases should be left outside its pale. I am far from advising indiscriminate operating. There are many things in surgery besides scalpels. But I do urge the need for hospitals close to the front, with every modern equipment, and with surgeons of resource and energy.

But for a surgeon this war between nations is only an incident in the war to which he has devoted his life—the war against disease. It is a curious reflection that whilst in the present war the base hospital has been given, if anything, an undue importance, in the other war it has been practically neglected. Our great hospitals are almost entirely field hospitals, planted right in the middle of the battle, and there we keep our patients till such time as they are to all intents and purposes cured. A very few convalescent homes will admit cases which still require treatment, but only a very few. The bulk of them expect their inmates to do the work of the establishment. Now, this is most unreasonable, for a country hospital is cheaper to build and should cost less to run than one in town, and in many cases the patients will recover in half the time. Our hospitals in London are always crowded, the waiting-lists mount up till it seems hopeless to attack them, and all the time it is because we have no base hospital down in the country to which our patients might be sent to recover. I wonder how long it will be before each of the great London hospitals has its own base down in the country, with its own motor ambulances and its own ambulance coaches to carry its patients in comfort by rail to surroundings where they could recover as can never be possible in the middle of the London slums ? And as to getting the staff to look after it, there would probably be a waiting-list for week-ends.

But there are more important considerations in this war than surgery, and one would have to be very blind not to perceive that this is a life-and-death struggle between Britain and Germany. The involvement of other nations is merely accidental. It is ourselves whom Germany is making this huge effort to crush, and but for one small circumstance she would have come within a measurable prospect of success. To swoop down

SOME CONCLUSIONS

on France through Belgium, to crush her in three weeks, to seize her fleet, and with the combined fleets of France and Germany to attack ours—that was the proposition, and who can say that it might not have succeeded ? The small circumstance which Germany overlooked was Belgium, and it is to the heroic resistance of Belgium that we owe the fact that the German advance has been stopped.

At the cost of the desolation of their own country, Belgium has perhaps saved the flag of Britain, for where would it have flown on the seas if Germany had won ? And at the very least she has saved us from a war beside which this is nothing—a war not now, but a few years hence, when she might have controlled half the Continent, and we should have stood alone. We owe an incalculable debt to Belgium, and we can only repay it by throwing into this war every resource that our country has to offer. For the only end which can bring peace to Europe is the total annihilation of Germany as a military and naval Power. What other terms can be made with a nation which regards its most solemn treaties as so much waste paper, which is bound by no conventions, and which delights in showing a callous disregard of all that forms the basis of a civilized society ? The only guarantees that we can take are that she has no ships of war, and that her army is only sufficient to police her frontier. The building of a war vessel or the boring of a gun must be regarded as a *casus belli*. Then, and then only, shall Europe be safe from the madness that is tearing her asunder.

But there is a wider view of this war than even that of Britain. We are not merely fighting to preserve the pre-eminence of our country; we are fighting for the civilization of the world. The victory of Germany would mean the establishment over the whole world of a military despotism such as the world has never seen. For if once the navy of Britain is gone, who else can stop her course? Canada, the United States, South America, would soon be vassals of her power—a power which would be used without scruple for her own material advantage. This is not a war between Germany and certain other nations; it is a war between Germany and civilization. The stake is not a few acres of land, but the freedom for which our fathers gave their lives.

Is there such a thing as neutrality in this war? Germany herself gave the answer when she invaded Belgium. It is the undoubted duty of many great nations, and of one before all others, to stand aside and not to enter the struggle; but to be neutral at heart, not to care whether the battle is won or lost, is impossible for any nation which values honour and truth above the passing advantages of worldly power. We do not ask America to fight on our side. This is our fight, and only Britain and her Allies can see it through. But we do ask for a sympathy which, while obeying the laws of neutrality to the last letter, will support us with a spirit which is bound by no earthly law, which will bear with us when in our difficult task we seem to neglect the interests of our friends, and will rejoice with us when, out of toil and sorrow, we have won a lasting peace.

This war is not of our choosing, and we shall never ask for peace. The sword has been thrust into our hands by a power beyond our own to defend from a relentless foe the flag which has been handed down to us unsullied through the ages, and to preserve for the world the freedom which is the proudest birthright of our race. When it is sheathed, the freedom of the world from the tyranny of man will have been secured.

Telegrams:
"Scholarly, Reg. London."
Telephone:
No. 1883 Mayfair.

41 and 43 Maddox Street,
Bond Street, London, W.
February, 1915.

Mr. Edward Arnold's
SPRING
ANNOUNCEMENTS, 1915.

A SURGEON IN BELGIUM.

By H. S. SOUTTAR, F.R.C.S.,
ASSISTANT SURGEON WEST LONDON HOSPITAL.

One Volume. Demy 8vo.

The author of this interesting and vivid narrative was one of the surgeons in charge of the British Field Hospital for Belgium, which began its work in Antwerp last September with 150 beds, and a staff of eight doctors and twenty nurses. On October 9th, in view of the German occupation, the hospital had to leave Antwerp. The retirement was effected in good order, over 100 wounded patients being removed in seven motor-buses. A fresh start was made at Furnes, where the hospital is still (January, 1915) at work, acting as the official Field Hospital of the Belgian Army. Furnes is only a few miles behind the trenches in the firing line, and the work of the hospital differed therefore considerably in character from that of the Base hospitals; in some cases important operations were carried out within an hour of the patient being wounded. The position of the hospital also made the work particularly exciting from a military point of view, and its independence of the British medical organisation brought up many novel problems of supply and maintenance. During his stay in Belgium the author had occasional opportunities of visiting several places already famous in the history of the war, such as Termonde, Malines, Purvies, and Ypres, and the scenes he witnessed are described with such graphic fidelity that the deep impression they made upon him at the time are conveyed to the reader without any loss of reality.

LONDON: EDWARD ARNOLD, 41 & 43 MADDOX STREET, W.

A SUMMER ON THE YENESEI.

By MAUD D. HAVILAND,
AUTHOR OF "THE WOOD PEOPLE," ETC.

With Numerous Illustrations from Photographs by the Author.

One Volume   Demy 8vo.   **10s. 6d. net.**

This is the account of a summer spent in unconventional surroundings among unconventional people. With three companions, the writer travelled two thousand miles down the mighty Yenesei River, and spent two months in a little pioneer settlement at the most northerly limit of civilization, among the simple Russian fisher-folk and the Siberian aborigines. Here, some weeks after its outbreak, news arrived of the war in Europe. The voyage home by sea was an adventurous one. The writer and one of her companions reached England in October, "like a pair of Rip van Winkles," knowing nothing but the barest facts about the war, which had then been raging for two months.

Miss Haviland is known as a keen naturalist and successful photographer of wild life, and the photographic illustrations are not the least interesting feature of the volume. But although the book is one which will appeal especially to nature lovers, it may be read with equal enjoyment by those who know nothing of natural history. It contains plenty of adventures, both comical and tragical, recounted in lively style; and introduces the reader to a number of characters, both human and feathered, that have not strayed into many previous books of travel.

THE WOOD PEOPLE: AND OTHERS.

By MAUD D. HAVILAND.

Illustrated by HARRY ROUNTREE.

Crown 8vo.   Cloth.   **5s. net.**

"Miss Maud D. Haviland is acknowledged as one of our most accomplished interpreters of the wild, and there is not a chapter in this latest selection of her nature stories that has failed to enthral us. The reader is simply compelled to be enmeshed in her wonderful imagination and look on at the lower animals living and loving, working and playing, as in some *comédie animale.*"—*Pall Mall Gazette.*

POULTRY HUSBANDRY.

By EDWARD BROWN, F.L.S.,

Late Hon. Sec. National Poultry Organisation Society; President International Association of Poultry Instructors and Investigators. Author of "Races of Domestic Poultry," "Poultry Fattening," etc.

Fully Illustrated. Demy 8vo. **8s. 6d. net.**

In no department of Animal Husbandry have greater changes taken place during the last two decades than the breeding of fowls and the production of eggs and poultry. Conditions and methods have completely altered. Systems formerly adopted have been abandoned or revolutionized, in many cases giving place to those which were previously unknown.

For the past year the author has been engaged upon an entirely new work, in which has been brought into one focus from his former works what is applicable to modern conditions, together with the result of practical experience, and research work of later years, dealing with the entire problem—productive, technical, and commercial. In it will be found a vast amount of new material, and special attention has been given to future developments, whether on extensive or intensive lines.

THE MAGNETIC COMPASS IN AIRCRAFT.

By Captain F. CREAGH OSBORNE, R.N.,

Superintendent of Compasses, Admiralty.

Post 8vo. With Transparent Protractor. Cloth. **2s. 6d. net.**

This little volume will be found indispensable by aviators, whose work has often been seriously handicapped for want of the information contained in it. The author's position as Director of Compasses at the Admiralty is a sufficient guarantee that the contents are eminently practical and lucid. A useful feature of the work is the inclusion, in a pocket, of a transparent circular protractor.

SCHOOL HYGIENE.

By Dr. W. B. DRUMMOND,

Author of "An Introduction to Child Study," etc.

Cloth. **3s. 6d.**

"Education is the guidance of growth. Everything which interferes with a child's growth interferes with the work of the teacher, and is, therefore, his concern." These words represent the point of view from which this book is written. Its special aim is to show how much enlightened teachers may do to promote their pupils' health both in and out of school. Common diseases and disorders are described with the object of explaining what can be done to avert the dangers which school life commonly entails.

Mr. Edward Arnold's Spring Announcements.

MEDICAL NURSING.
By A. S. WOODWARK, M.D., M.R.C.P.,
Lecturer on Medical Nursing and Physician to the Royal Waterloo Hospital and Miller General Hospital for South-East London; Medical Tutor to King's College Hospital.

335 *pages, and* 68 *Illustrations.*   *Crown 8vo.*   **4s. 6d. net.**

The author, in addition to giving clear instructions in modern methods of nursing, has endeavoured to supply in a concise form all the information needed by a nurse in regard to the illnesses from which her patients may be suffering.

One feature in which this work differs from most books on nursing is that the symptoms and treatment of each disease are outlined so that the nurse is enabled to follow the line of treatment ordered by the physician, and can thus the more intelligently carry out the clearly described details of nursing.

The whole field of Medical Nursing is dealt with. Massage, which is now an important branch of medical treatment, has had the attention which its growing importance deserves. Full instructions are given for dealing with the common emergencies which are likely to arise, instructions being given which will enable the nurse to carry out treatment pending the arrival of the physician. The subject of Invalid Cookery is fully discussed.

SURGICAL AFTER-TREATMENT.
By ALAN H. TODD, M.B., M.S., F.R.C.S.,
Surgical Registrar and Tutor, Guy's Hospital.

Crown 8vo.   *Illustrated.*   **About 4s. 6d. net.**

Whether or not an operation is successful depends, not only upon the skill of the surgeon and the method of carrying out the operation, but upon the care which is subsequently bestowed upon the patient and the method of after-treatment employed.

It will be readily admitted that the end of the operation frequently marks the commencement of the surgeon's anxiety. Careful after-treatment will often bring through safely the most hopeless case, while neglect or lack of care will render void the result of the most skilful surgeon's efforts.

The author has made full use of his opportunities, and here gives the benefit of his successful experience at one of the large Metropolitan hospitals.

SEVENTY YEARS OF IRISH LIFE.
By W. R. Le FANU.

A New, Popular Edition.   *Paper Covers,* **1s. net ;**   *Cloth,* **2s. net.**

"It would be difficult to find any single volume containing such a multitude of capital stories between its covers."—*Daily Telegraph.*

"This book is a feast of amusing anecdote. It will delight all readers—English and Scotch no less than Irish, Nationalists no less than Unionists, Roman Catholics no less than Orangemen."—*Times.*

NEW NOVELS.

HIS ENGLISH WIFE
(SEINE ENGLISCHE FRAU).
By RUDOLPH STRATZ.
6s.

It is thought that this novel may possess special interest at the present time as showing how our English character and way of living appear when seen " Through German Eyes." The book is carefully constructed to bring out the contrast, at as many points as possible, between the decadence attributed by the author to the English nation, and the patriotic idealism which he claims for the Germans. His obvious sincerity and earnestness of purpose, and the fact that his book had won a wide popularity among his countrymen before the war broke out, are a sufficient guarantee that we have here an unusually favourable opportunity of seeing ourselves as others see us.

BILLIE'S MOTHER.
By MARY J. H. SKRINE,
AUTHOR OF "A STEPSON OF THE SOIL," "A ROMANCE OF THE SIMPLE," ETC.
Crown 8vo. **6s.**

Mrs. Skrine is noted for the fidelity of her studies of English country life, and for the success with which she compasses that particularly rare and difficult thing, the creation of a living peasant in fiction. In her new novel she goes further afield and takes in a wider horizon generally than in her previous books, thus offering more satisfactory enjoyment to her readers.

This story is a study of an English peasant woman, who in difficult, unfamiliar, and conflicting circumstances, is still swayed and guided by her inherited and racial instincts and codes. It tells of her mistakes and her wisdom, of her fears, hopes, and outlook, and of the conflict of the two great strands of love in such a woman—for the man and for the child. Her disastrous husband, his sins and sorrows; her baby son Billie, his puzzlement and point of view; his refreshing sister Lickle; a Scotch nurse; a family lawyer, John Rixby; and last, but not least, the old mother, Susan Rogers, and her contributions to the solution of the main problem—all find their places in the plot and movement of the narrative.

Its scene is laid in Australia, then in the New Forest country, with an episode not unimportant in an old Scotch country house. We will not further reveal the story, which, it is hoped, will carry on the reader with a natural motion through its difficult and poignant developments.

Mr. Edward Arnold's New Books.

NEW NOVELS.

A BRILLIANT NOVEL BY THE AUTHOR OF "TANTE."

THE ENCOUNTER.

By ANNE DOUGLAS SEDGWICK,
AUTHOR OF "TANTE," "FRANKLIN KANE," "AMABEL CHANNICE," ETC.

6s.

" 'The Encounter' is a striking story. It is a novel that reveals an intimate and careful study of the German mind from a woman's point of view, and, being at the same time an extremely ably-written book, it should find many interested readers at the present moment."—*Morning Post.*

"The individuality, even the idiosyncrasy, of each character in this story is drawn with such lucidity and precision that one gets something of the impression of a group of statuary. The creative artistry of it all fills one with profound admiration. This is a story of quite exceptional power and interest, and no one who loves good literature should miss it."—*Pall Mall Gazette.*

"It is impossible to leave a page unread—many pages are worth re-reading again and again. The book is full of beauty and wisdom."—*Westminster Gazette.*

"This is a book which it is impossible not to finish and admire."—*Country Life.*

"A brilliant conception of the interplay of temperament such as has ever been the theme of real novelists."—*Athenæum.*

"The portrait of a small German watering-place is delicious, and throughout the writing is as firm as it is supple. The story has the fine intention and broadly designed setting which we expect from such an artist as Miss Sedgwick."—*Manchester Guardian.*

"A novel that is brilliant, a novel that grows all the greater in retrospect."
—*Boston Evening Transcript.*

LOCKETT'S LEA.

By SIBELL VANSITTART.

6s.

"A clever novel of hereditary tendencies."—*Spectator.*

"An amazingly interesting story of the life of a girl who is born to wickedness by reason of the sins of both her father and her mother. The book is exceptionally clever."—*Globe.*

"Well worth reading."—*Observer.*

NEW NOVELS.

IN THE CITY OF UNDER.

By EVELYNE RYND,
AUTHOR OF "MRS. GREEN."

Second Impression. **6s.**

"The story is a medley of mystery, allegory, fairy fiction, and wholesome philosophy, so skilfully blended that the whole assumes an aspect of vivid reality. The effect is one of complete novelty. We do not know anything that quite equalls the story in this quality of originality. Its freshness and absolute unconventionality gives it an irresistible charm."—*Pall Mall Gazette.*

"'In the City of Under' is a charming book."—*Times.*

"Miss Evelyne Rynd's new book, 'In the City of Under,' is published by Mr. Edward Arnold, who is, in my opinion, one of the very best judges of fiction among the publishers. Miss Rynd won her position years ago with that most excellent and living book, 'Mrs. Green.' 'In the City of Under' thoroughly deserves and richly rewards careful reading."—*British Weekly.*

"A story quite delightfully out of the common."—*Tatler.*

ALIENS.

By WILLIAM McFEE.

6s.

"Mr. McFee begins with a tremendous incident, and then the story harks back and ultimately leads up to it again. In the meantime he gains and maintains our interest both in the story and the manner of its telling. Perhaps he has never read Mr. Conrad, but it would be surprising to be assured of that. It is not only that the broken, indirect method, the seeing through others' eyes, alternates with simple and direct narration very much as the author of 'Chance' might have devised it, but the phrases are sometimes almost familiar. 'Well, what do you think he asked me for? Nothing less than fifty pounds. He seemed to have a mania for fifty pounds.' This is splendid, and Mr. Conrad might have written it."—*Manchester Guardian.*

"There is an indefinable charm in 'Aliens.'"—*Evening Standard.*

"This narrative is extraordinarily simple, direct, and gripping."—*Liverpool Daily Post.*

"There are some books which make you say, 'Here is literature—whatever this man writes is worth reading.' Such a book is 'Aliens.'"—*Christian Globe.*

NEW NOVELS.

THE WISE VIRGINS.
By LEONARD WOOLF,
AUTHOR OF "THE VILLAGE IN THE JUNGLE."

6s.

"The story is extraordinarily clever and amusing, and it certainly leaves one rather agape."—*Pall Mall Gazette.*

"The story is rich in closely-studied details of character and manners, and here and there are emotional scenes of singular art."—*The Times.*

"Mr. Woolf is going to be another of the novelists who count. 'The Wise Virgins' is notable chiefly for the smartness of its dialogue. The talk is not only witty; it is really good."—*Scotsman.*

"It is only to those who can stand tragedy and like plain speaking that the book can be recommended. To them it can be recommended very strongly."—*Country Life.*

THE HOLE OF THE PIT.
By ADRIAN ROSS (ARTHUR R. ROPES).

6s.

"Seldom since the death of Edgar Allan Poe has there been published a book more uncanny, yet stamped with greater verisimilitude than 'The Hole of the Pit.' Mr. A. R. Ropes has conceived a weird yet enthralling plot."—*Yorkshire Post.*

"Mr. Ropes skilfully blends the weird and repulsive in incident and loca colour with the tender glow of first love."—*Occult Review.*

"The author is to be congratulated on the skill and taste with which he insinuates horrors rather than describes them."—*Birmingham Post.*

THE RECOILING FORCE.
By A. M. CHAMPNEYS,
AUTHOR OF "BRIDE ELECT."

6s.

"This story has much better claim to attention than that of merely possessing a clever label. It is a story of the liveliest interest, in which three very different characters are skilfully drawn."—*Liverpool Daily Post.*

"It is a good novel, and the characterization is excellent."—*Yorkshire Post.*

RECOLLECTIONS OF BAR AND BENCH.

By the Right Hon. VISCOUNT ALVERSTONE, G.C.M.G., K.B.

With Portraits, and numerous Sketches by the late SIR FRANK LOCKWOOD.

Third Impression. *Demy 8vo.* **12s. 6d. net.**

"A book which is a mine of ripe experience and sound suggestion. In its condensation, its contempt for the unreal and the unnecessary, its characteristic sanity and thorough breadth of view, above all its plainness and restraint of speech, it reminds us of one great predecessor of the author's on the English Bench, and his name was Francis Bacon."—*Pall Mall Gazette.*

"Lord Alverstone's recollections are the story of professional success rarely—if, indeed, ever—equalled. They will be studied, and with profit, by every young and ambitious barrister."—*The Times.*

"A book full of wisdom that is not altogether professional, and much richer in humour than you would think at first sight."—*Morning Post.*

"As his work has brought him into touch with a great many representative details of our national life, its arts and sciences, manufactures, hygiene, and politics, his pages are interesting to everyone."—*Evening Standard.*

"Lord Alverstone's achievements in politics, in athletics, and in music fill other chapters in this well-arranged book of 'Recollections,' which every man in the profession, young and old—and especially the young—will want to read for himself."—*Law Journal.*

"This volume will make a wide appeal by reason of its general interest and of the judicial wisdom and shrewd knowledge of human nature which manifest themselves in every chapter."—*Guardian.*

"Must prove of great interest to lawyers and laymen alike."—*Liverpool Daily Post.*

"Good and interesting books of reminiscences are especially welcome just now when the depressing 'fog of war' lies over us all. They help to take us out of ourselves, and so there will be a warm and wide welcome for Lord Alverstone's 'Recollections.'"—*Daily Chronicle.*

GERMANY AND THE NEXT WAR.

By General F. VON BERNHARDI.

Popular Edition, **2s.** *net, paper ;* **2s. 6d.** *net, cloth.*

This is the great "Bernhardi" book—the author's latest work in its complete form.

Mr. Edward Arnold's New Books.

DAYS OF MY YEARS.

By Sir MELVILLE MACNAGHTEN, C.B.

With Portrait.   One Volume.   Demy 8vo.   **12s. 6d. net.**

"A great debt is due to Mr. Arnold, for Sir Melville was at one time adamant in his refusal to write his memoirs, and if he had persisted in his decision many excellent things would have been lost to us."—*Weekly Dispatch.*

"Those who imagine that only French police officials can write good books about their work will be surprised at the readableness of Sir Melville's volume."—*Globe.*

"A varied and most human book."—*Observer.*

"A fascinating volume, and written with a grace and a gay gentleness that make, as it were, a fragrant border to the garden of guilt in which the debonair 'detective's' feats were accomplished."—*Referee.*

"Sir Melville's book is engrossing."—*Sketch.*

"Sir Melville MacNaghten strikes us as a man who has enjoyed his life's work extremely well, and his readers, if only they have the normal appetite for crime, will enjoy his book."—*Saturday Review.*

"As full of human interest as it is easy and colloquial in its style."—*Daily Graphic.*

THE COMPLETE SPORTSMAN.

By HARRY GRAHAM,

AUTHOR OF "THE PERFECT GENTLEMAN," "RUTHLESS RHYMES FOR HEARTLESS HOMES," ETC.

Illustrated by LEWIS BAUMER.

One Volume.   *Crown 8vo.*   **6s.**

"For a good laugh let me recommend 'The Complete Sportsman.' Captain Harry Graham has conferred a blessing upon hundreds of new readers beside those many thousands who have already stood up to give him a cheer with 'The Perfect Gentleman' held tightly in their hands. The sportsman who can get on without it will be dreary company."—*Tatler.*

"The better the sportsman, and the more he knows about game of all kinds, the more will he enjoy this delicious caricature of sporting reminiscences."—*Queen.*

PAGES FROM AN UNWRITTEN DIARY.

By Sir CHARLES VILLIERS STANFORD,
Mus.Doc., D.C.L., LL.D.

With Photogravure Portrait and other Illustrations. Demy 8vo.
12s. 6d. net.

" This volume is quite the best thing of its kind that English musical autobiography can show. Sir Charles has met many distinguished men, seen them all with very clear eyes, and preserved many admirable vignettes for us. It would be hard to find a book so full of good stories, many of them of the best Irish kind."—*Nation.*

" A volume full of the most attractive anecdotes."—*Evening Standard.*

" One of the best books of reminiscences we have ever read."—*Outlook.*

" From almost every page we could pick out a plum "—*Queen.*

" We would open our notice of this delightful volume with a word of assurance to the general reader. It is certainly written by a distinguished musician, but little knowledge of music or musicians is needed for its appreciation. The same admirably catholic taste which enables him to appreciate Brahms and Wagner, Bach and Offenbach, Gluck and Johann Strauss, is shown in his outlook on humanity, and is one of the chief charms of the book."—*Spectator.*

FRIENDS AND MEMORIES.

By MAUDE VALERIE WHITE.

One Volume. Demy 8vo. **12s. 6d. net.**

" A human document of the most enthralling interest. Though we all know Miss White as the composer of many magnificent songs, it is rather as a happy optimist, an intensely human personage, a genial critic, and a perfect raconteuse that she shows herself in this witty, humorous, actual, vivid, sparkling book."—*Daily Telegraph.*

" One of the most interesting and delightful memoirs I have read for a long time. It is quite a wonderful example of the fascination of a sense of humour. Miss White is never dull. She writes naturally and delightfully, and her Great Folk are just as human and simple as she is herself."—*Tatler.*

" Never has it been my good fortune to read so many pages that are filled with what I can only call the fragrance of life. Sorrows and troubles Miss White has known in abundance, but she steadfastly refuses to dwell upon anything but the joy of living and the kindness of her many friends. This splendid way of regarding the world is one of the qualities that has made her welcome and more than welcome wherever she goes ; it is also the quality that gives an almost unique distinction to her volume of reminiscences."—*Punch.*

ADVENTURES AMONG WILD FLOWERS.

By JOHN TREVENA.

With Illustrations. One Volume. Large Crown 8vo. **7s. 6d. net.**

" A book of very great attractiveness. A very discursive book it is, with much autobiographical revelation and opinions on all things in heaven and earth. Running through this collection of essays we find, however, a pleasing and refreshing survey of many flowers and plants which will be dear to all lovers of gardens, of whom I am one. Yet most of all in Mr. Trevena's book do I care for the many anecdotes."—*The Sphere.*

" This volume is another nail hammered into the coffin-lid of dry-as-dust natural history. Mr. Trevena's book is as engrossing and knowledgable as any of that growing series of nature books which, in order of merit, stand only one shelf below that on which repose the masterpieces of Jefferies and Mr. W. H. Hudson."—*Pall Mall Gazette.*

YE SUNDIAL BOOK.

By T. GEOFFREY W. HENSLOW, M.A.

With 400 Illustrations. Royal 8vo. Handsomely bound, **10s. 6d. net.**

" All lovers of sundials—and what garden of any size is complete without one? —will welcome this beautiful book with enthusiasm. Here we have between 300 and 400 delineations of sundials in their surroundings, each a little work of art in itself."—*Evening Standard.*

" A very charming book on a delightful subject. As a guide to choice in design of sundials this unique collection of illustrations is invaluable to amateurs as well as to architects and garden designers."—*Liverpool Daily Post.*

THE PROMENADE TICKET: A LAY RECORD OF CONCERTS.

By A. H. SIDGWICK,
AUTHOR OF "WALKING ESSAYS."

Crown 8vo. **3s. 6d. net.**

" A witty and delightful book, full of genial criticism of music, music-lovers, and would-be music-lovers."—*Spectator.*

" What the Upton Letters—owing, perhaps, to a certain grandiosity—just failed to do for literature and the amenities, this book, in a more unbuttoned way, easily compasses for music."—*The Times.*

" It is a criticism which will be read with relish by every music-lover, and not least by the professional musician. 'The Promenade Ticket' is emphatically a book to be enjoyed."—*Musical News.*

LONDON: EDWARD ARNOLD, 41 & 43 MADDOX STREET, W.

www.ingramcontent.com/pod-product-compliance
Lightning Source LLC
Chambersburg PA
CBHW032125160426
43197CB00008B/525